WISDOM ON
HER TONGUE

WISDOM ON HER TONGUE

Tips for Getting Back Your Weekends &
Holidays & Learning to Communicate
Effectively in Marriage

LEXY SAUVÉ

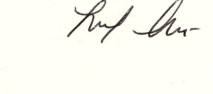

NEW
CHRISTENDOM
PRESS

Hardback ISBN: 978-1-964404-05-9
Ebook ISBN: 978-1-964404-06-6
Library of Congress Control Number: 2025909067

For Brian

*Thank you for being patient and
charitable and forgiving toward me as
I've learned to walk in all the things
I've written about in this book.*

CONTENTS

GET BACK YOUR WEEKENDS

By the end of Proverbs 31, we stand back and marvel at King Lemuel's lyrical model of the virtuous woman. She is the excellent wife, more precious than jewels (10). She has the heart of her husband, who trusts her (11), knowing that she will do him good and not harm all her days (12). Her industry is marvelous (13–16), her arms clothed with strength (17). She diligently labors in her household from early morning (15) and even toils into the night (18). Far from an anxious bundle of raw nerves, ready to explode at the slightest provocation, she laughs at the time to come, her raiment woven of strength and dignity (25). Her mouth knows wisdom, and kindness is always to be found on her tongue (26). The result of all this glory? Her people bless her name and praise her: "Many women have done excellently, but you surpass them all" (28–29).

What would happen if we built her foil? If we described her polar opposite—the anti-Proverbs 31 woman? How would we sketch her character?

She is a poor wife, as common as lead. She has firmly secured the antipathy of her husband, who trusts only that she will bring him pain and harm all her days—which he finds himself wishing were short. Her industry is lackluster, her arms clothed with laziness. She rises late and neglects home and hearth, staying up late to mindlessly scroll her social media feeds. Her nerves are the constant companion of all those unfortunates who must live with her, ready to explode at the merest touch of stress. Her raiment is moodiness and disrespect. Her mouth knows sarcasm; battery acid is on her tongue. The result of this infamy? Her people curse her name and hope to escape her: "Many women have done excellently, but you are certainly not one of them."

What kind of home would such a woman make around her? What kind of marriage? What kind of children? What kind of church, community, and even nation? Unfortunately, we see the answer all around us, as women like this are no mere caricature living on the printed page alone. They are almost comically easy to find. Why is this? For one reason, our culture has taken to manufacturing them with seeming deliberateness. What is feminism but a factory for mass-producing loud, disrespectful, nagging women—the kind of women a man would do anything to escape?

In Titus 2, the Apostle Paul urges godly older women to teach younger women not to fall for it. The women of God, Paul says, are not to be drunk with rudeness, tearing their homes down around their own heads, but rather experts in loving husbands, raising children, and making homes that would crown the Christian community with glory. This is so serious, Paul warns, that the very Word of God will be reviled if they fail in this charge.

That's what this book is about. In the following chapters, my wife pulls no punches, urging you further up and further in on the winding pathway to glory—to become a crown on your husband's head rather than cancer in his bones. It's a book about getting back your weekends and holidays—you know, the ones you've been losing to days-long fits of the grumps, pointless fights with your husband, and other sinful immaturities. It's a book to wound you with the wounds of a friend, a sister who loves you enough to look you in the eye and say, "This has got to stop" to the things that are only hurting you and those around you.

One last thing you should know before you continue: Lexy lives out what she writes in these pages. I've known this woman since we met in the library of North Layton Junior High during lunch period. Both of us have had our share of growing and maturing to do; when you get married at 19 and 20, these things come with the wedding rings. We've lost our fair share of nights and weekends to silly fights. We've had to learn what it is to be a husband and to be a wife. We've had to wrestle our own flesh and forgive one another. Through it all, I can say without a doubt that my wife is a crown. Her children (and there are seven of them so far, by the way) rise up and call her blessed.

I pray this book will bless you and yours, encourage you in the race you're in the midst of running, and urge you on to glory.

BRIAN SAUVÉ

CHAPTER I

WHY A BOOK ABOUT COMMUNICATION?

Growing up in a military family, we moved approximately every 6.32 months. Not really, but it sure felt like it. Because of this, we logged many hours on the road, making countless treks across America, living on both coasts multiple times, and taking a few harrowing, icy journeys across Canada. My parents were good at keeping my younger brother and me busy in the back of my dad's Ford pickup. I always loved to nest down into the tiny corner of the bench seat with a stack of road trip books and my down pillow; I still associate *The Yearling* with our time spent driving across New Mexico. My mom often had audiobooks for us as well and even bought a tiny TV that my dad harnessed to the center console so we could watch *Old Yeller* on repeat (this was before cars with built-in televisions, let alone iPads). I love cooking to '80s classic rock to this day simply because it reminds me of my dad trying to stay awake through the white tundra of Canada for day ten of a two-week drive.

Even with all these forms of entertainment, there was simply so much time on the road that we didn't lack in quiet time. After what felt like hours of us counting clouds through the vistas of Wyoming or admiring the distant plateaus of the uniquely beautiful Southwest, my mom would occasionally ask my dad, "What are you thinking about?"

"Nothing."

"Nothing? *How* are you thinking about nothing?"

My dad would laugh and say something like, "I don't know. I go into my nothing box and just think about…*nothing*!"

From the back seat, it was always clear to me that my mom wanted to chat and was hoping my dad would provide some conversational fodder. It's funny to reflect on this conversation as a grown and married woman now because I've had the same exact conversation many times with my husband and in many contexts. I'm sure many of us ladies have as well. It's funny because even after all these years of digging around my own mind, I still haven't found my nothing box, even when I desperately wish I could. I have boxes for all the connections I've made through the landscape of books I've journeyed through (that I want to tell my husband about), boxes for things I want to cook but don't have the time to right now (but I think my husband would like), boxes for the things I need to remember to buy for the kids before next season (but I need to talk to my husband about), boxes for useless things like all the names of the Farrow & Ball paint I want to add to my house (and talk to my husband about)—I have boxes and boxes of things rattling around in there, but I certainly don't have a nothing box.

In His wisdom, God created women to be *communica-*

tive creatures. Just think of the tasks in which Paul would have the older women train the younger in Titus 2:3–5:

> Older women likewise … are to teach what is good, and so train the young women to love their husbands and children, to be self-controlled, pure, working at home, kind, and submissive to their own husbands, that the word of God may not be reviled.

These are relational tasks; tasks that require us to spend a lot of time communicating with others, often trying to get a gauge of mental, physical, spiritual, and emotional morale. "How was work today? Are you tired? Do you need a snack? It's bedtime. Do you need a snack? A back scratch? A wool blanket? Another snack?" If our people are sick, we communicate with them about it so we can wrap them up in the special turquoise sick quilt Great Grandma made and tuck a heating pad behind their back. If our people have had a rough week, we communicate with them about it so we can cook up their favorite meal. If our husband has a heavy workload for a few weeks, we communicate about what the most helpful things would be to do for him.

Think about it. If we never *talked* to the people God has called us to serve, we literally wouldn't know *how* to best serve them! We genuinely *want* our kids to tell us what helps them fall asleep best when they're sick and we *want* to know our husband's thoughts about mealtimes (maybe). We *want* to know our mother-in-law's favorite desserts so we can make one of them for her birthday. We *want* to know how our kids are doing in catechism class so we can set them up for success at home. As women, success in our job depends upon communication.

Commenting on this design feature, I once heard a wise,

older pastor's wife say that because women like to talk about their thoughts and emotions, especially with their husbands, they had *better* master the skills of communicating well.

Why?

A theme you will see come up often in this short book is that the power of life and death is in the tongue (Prov. 18:21). If we want to share our every thought and desire with our husbands while being respectful and encouraging, then we must understand that the *way* we communicate can either build up our households or tear them down (Prov. 14:1). Like Eve, we could lead our husbands into sin with our tongues, or, like Lady Wisdom (Prov. 8), we could build up our husbands, spurring them on to be bold men of God and leaders of our homes, churches, and culture. It is the latter that a God-fearing woman certainly desires.

It's my prayer that this book would be a mental training course that you can run through to set yourself and your marriage up for helpful communication habits. Learn how to put out the petty fires, stop them in the first place, and get back your weekends and holidays from all the ridiculous things you used to fuss and fight about. What would happen if Christian women everywhere mastered these habits? If marriages were marked by these patterns of maturity? If Christian women knew what it was to have a gentle and quiet spirit? If Christian marriages were known for the joy and contentment of Christ? These habits are not easy, but they are worthy of our zealous effort.

Chapter 2

Five-Paragraph Essays & Self-Control

One of the most helpful things my mother did to prepare me for marriage was teaching me the basics of the five-paragraph essay. I can remember sitting at our wooden table practicing the formula over and over again: introductory paragraph with a thesis statement, three supporting paragraphs demonstrating the validity of my thesis, and a concluding paragraph summarizing the essay. I can remember pulling out the blue book she used to teach from to refer to when I needed to make something coherent out of a messy knot of thoughts.

Throughout high school and college, this simple formula continued to help me succeed in my studies and find enjoyment in my work, bringing complex and tangled issues into clarity. I've always loved writing, even from my earliest memories, and expressing my thoughts hasn't often been a struggle for me, but the structure this formula provided gave me even more confidence in organizing my thoughts and opinions on a wide variety of subjects—spooky stories; arts and entertainment interviews I'd write for my university's newspaper; poems; and essays on Shakespeare's sonnets, Anne Bradstreet's brilliance as a mother and author, or Pascal's faith, just to name a few.

When I was a young bride, I had no idea what a gift this language arts lesson would be in learning how to communicate with my husband. It may feel hyper-logical, cold, or distant to think about your emotions this way, but to be honest, most people probably need *more* distance, not less, from their emotions. It's often the case that you have to back up from your emotions a good distance and think for a moment in order to accurately handle them, let alone communicate them to someone else.

Maybe it simply hasn't occurred to you to interrogate your emotions. Maybe your mother didn't teach you the five-paragraph essay. Maybe you've been taught to believe everything you feel is true. Hint: It's not! Even if your feelings *are* ringing in harmony with reality, that by itself doesn't mean you always have the wisdom to know what to *do* about how you feel, or how to communicate your feelings and thoughts in a way that maintains your integrity while also building up, correcting, or edifying your listeners. Maybe the only example of marriage you've ever seen was riddled with communication that manipulated others and brimmed with unkindness and bitterness that has rotted away all the life and marrow in the relationship. Maybe you truly wouldn't know how to give a man a proper compliment if your life depended on it.

If this is you, don't be discouraged. God is in the business of starting new generational legacies, and with His help, you can become a productive communicator of your emotions. It is rather humbling and hard to admit that you don't know how to do something correctly—but if this is you, I'd encourage you to start right there. The next time you're having a disagreement, express quickly and early to your husband that your desire is to grow in communicating in a kind way, so ask him to be patient. My husband often says that when you do this, it is quick to kindle mercy in the other person. It also takes a weight off your back and prevents you from succumbing to perfectionism and freezing up, which, ironically, often leads to you giving full vent to your anger in the long run, all in the name of, "Well, I messed this up anyways! This can't make it much worse."

You don't have to have perfect eye contact or express the proper level of emotion in your voice. Sometimes quick and flat expression, with a true heart desire to not blow up and sin, is okay. You will grow, get better at expression, and your body language will fall in line with obedience. If you're waiting for the day when you can communicate hard things in ways that aren't awkward, you're going to be waiting … well, forever.

Once you have that out of the way, I think you'll find helpful tools in the five-paragraph essay formula that can help you analyze, correct, and express your emotions profitably to others. Let's get more specific and you'll see what I mean.

First, a five-paragraph essay opens with an introductory paragraph. That paragraph is essentially a statement about what you believe, as well as the evidence you will elaborate on in the body of the essay to support your belief. For example, "I believe we should always eat tacos on Friday *because* everyone loves tacos, they're quick to make, and Mom is tired by the end of the week." Making yourself give *specific* expression to your emotions like this is a fast way to show where you may be thinking unreasonably. If you can't express *specifically* why you're annoyed with your husband, you likely have zero right to feel the way you do. "I'm just annoyed at you tonight because I am" is immature reasoning, and, at the very least, you ought to grow up out of communicating that way, even if you do feel that way at first. Or maybe you genuinely need a little more time to sit on how you're feeling *so that you can* communicate profitably. That's a good game plan as well.

Having supporting evidence for why you feel the way you do is especially essential when communicating volatile content to others. "I'm annoyed that you got to go out with friends last weekend while I was home with sick children." This is getting a little closer to a more helpful way of communicating, but further investigation will determine with even more clarity whether the speaker has a *genuine* right to feel the way she does. This is where elaborating on evidence in supporting paragraphs comes into play.

Think about your evidence. Maybe it's true that your husband went golfing all day last Saturday and you stayed home all day because the kids were sick, but ladies, it's crucial that you don't stop here. Don't overlook glaring evidence that will further help you in the mystery of untangling your emotions and living according to reality.

It may also be true that your husband came home with your favorite dinner and a tub of your favorite ice cream. He watched a movie with the kids and told you to take a bath to relax. He tidied up the house after he sent you to bed early so you wouldn't have to play as much catch-up on housework. I find that when we are looking through the lens of our gut reactions instead of reality, we overlook many mercies and kindnesses. We can tend to *magnify* the things that justify our moodiness, all the while *minimizing* any exonerating evidence on the side of the object of our moodiness.

If you don't have accurate supporting evidence to show your feelings are justified, crinkle up those thoughts and throw them into the nearest trash can. Don't spend any more time with them. Once you have determined that certain thoughts or feelings you have been entertaining are not leading you into truth, peace, kindness, and joy, then you need to realize that spending *more* time in endless analysis isn't the answer. You don't need to keep turning those thoughts over in your mind, calling a friend to chat about them for an hour or two, or anything else. At this point, instead, toss them into the trash. They're of no value to you in this untrue form anyway; they're only causing you to waste time and energy. Firmly escorting your emotions out of the room when they are trying to swindle you isn't the sign of an emotionally stunted woman, but of a *mature* woman.

Death and life are in the power of the tongue, so it really is good to force your thoughts, emotions, and the words you use into a structure that allows critical evaluation. Communicating our emotions is dangerous work. Just like practicing the fundamentals of gun safety is critical to protect those around you when handling a firearm, practicing proper self-control when handling your emotions will prevent negligently wounding and destroying the things you love.

But what if you feel like you *do* have evidence and justification for why you feel the way you do? Keep thinking clearly: Is it biblical evidence? You can't always provide two or three witnesses to your husband's behavior behind closed doors, but has it *happened* at least two or three times? Is it a serious issue or a minor one? Is it habitual or something that happened once? Does he have men speaking into his life on this issue, or is it something unlikely to be dealt with unless you respectfully bring it to his attention? If, upon weighing these kinds of questions, you determine that you need to respectfully bring a concern to your husband, make sure you can do so with specificity and accuracy—offering the times and places that you saw the concern unfolding. Here is an example: "You have gotten drunk every holiday in the last year, and any time we are at a work party you also get drunk. I'm concerned about this habit and wanted to bring it to your attention."

If you can't do that, if you can't get specific, sit on it a bit. Pray about it. Ask God to bring clarity or to bring any needed correction to your husband directly or through other authorities in his life. It's hard to go wrong if you sit on it a bit longer, *as long as* you pray along the way and aren't being passive about genuine sin.

After getting specific about your emotions and what you believe has justly caused them, be constructive about providing recommendations to help. It's reasonable to *ask* for something, but 100 percent unreasonable to assume your husband learned telepathy overnight. If this is you, it's simply unkind and you need to stop. Let me give an example: "Sure, I don't mind if you go play golf with your friends today. It's a good Saturday for it since the kids are sick and we can't really all go do something together. Do you mind bringing home dinner tonight so I can relax a bit today though? I didn't sleep super well with the toddler next to me last night." Only an unreasonable husband himself would deny such a wise, cheerful petition.

It is often at this step, where the help and reasons for the help are being communicated, that women give way to crying. Please know, I am not above tears. I've had many a long, sleepless season where crying almost felt like my main form of autopilot. The Lord knows that these times can be very hard. A good husband knows the challenges facing a woman in various seasons of life and sympathizes tenderly with her. But it is important to note, with love and understanding, that all of this doesn't mean you *have* to cry, okay? There are other options, like learning to laugh at the chaos God seems to entrust you with. I know, I know...not always easy. But the Lord is on our side, and we can do hard things. Amen?

If what you're observing in your spouse is less about your emotional reactions to issues and more about specific and habitual sins that you genuinely see, provide recommendations to show your husband you are serious about being his helper. Maybe you feel concerned because your husband comes home from work and immediately sits at the computer to catch up on emails and then hops back online after dinner. The kids aren't getting catechized because of it, and the conversation in the home is lacking. If it were me, I'd probably offer to let him stay longer at work if that would help make the home a predominantly work-free zone after dinner. I'd ask if he needs any new resources or books for discipling the kids that you could pick up for him. Maybe even do some of your own research and recommend a title.

Be a help, but don't be pushy. And do leave the ball in his court.

Finally, at the end of the conversation, I like to practice offering a one-sentence summary of how I'm feeling, why, and what could help the situation. Often, if I can't come up with this in one sentence, I know my emotions may not be valid, or at the very least, I need to sit on them a little longer in search of clarity.

When I'm doing this, I will quite literally write down my thoughts, even if it's in brief and in a bullet point form, and I'd encourage you to do the same. It's rare that circumstances require you to react in the moment, even if your tiredness, hormone level, hunger, or past hurt is demanding you do so. You are the boss of yourself, not your fleshly desires (Prov. 25:28). Refer to this list right before going into your conversation to protect yourself from saying untrue and unhelpful things. Even if things don't go fully as planned, going through the work of learning to interrogate and better communicate your thoughts is still going to benefit your marriage in the long run. Practice will strengthen the muscles you need to turn the volume down on the lies and unhelpful things your emotions would love to vomit out without restraint—and the muscles you need to communicate what ought to be said, clearly and with love. With God's help, you can get better and better at communicating profitably over time if you're willing to put in the practice.

Chapter 3

Big Emotions

One of the biggest kindnesses my husband has given me has been helping me acknowledge and navigate hormonal fluctuations. These cyclical ups and downs are part of every woman's life. God created our bodies with this design feature, and He called it very good. It has been helpful to hear my husband reinforce that it is *indeed* very good that God made me this way. It is a means of health and life. I know he doesn't look down upon me for this aspect of my nature, but rather delights in how God created me. But on the flip side, he has not once allowed me to be bossed around by my big emotions.

It's important to acknowledge up front that we are Christians, and because we are Christians, we can admit that our physical bodies affect our emotional and spiritual state and vice versa. My favorite example is Proverbs 17:22, which says, "A joyful heart is good medicine, but a crushed spirit dries up the bones." Literally, everything you experience in life—physically, mentally, emotionally, and spiritually—could be more enjoyable to you if you simply cultivated a cheerful disposition. It's obvious to everyone that a nasty attitude makes a bad day worse, but it's often hard for us to admit the opposite.

Because of this interplay between body and spirit, it's important to acknowledge that our hormonal fluctuations really *do* make us feel worse some of the time. The same can be true of mental and physical stressors. It's not just the overly anxious person who gets a tummy ache, but also the person faithfully living out their duties. The everyday good works of life take their toll on all our bodies. It's not *just* all in your head or made up or silly.

When I've experienced these realities in my own life, they have come as divinely appointed reminders that my very being is dependent upon Him for every breath—and that the way He provides physical and mental health is sometimes through extra naps, cheeseburgers, and a patient husband. We are learning our own limits in the schoolroom of God's providence; these things are appointed by God. They are creaturely boundaries, given by God to kindly remind us of our own frame. Seasons of pregnancy, miscarriage, illness, intense physical and mental stress (like a move or caring for a dying family member), postpartum, and menopause are just a few seasons of a woman's life in which what's physically happening inside her may leave her feeling like a grumpy stranger to herself and those around her.

Even though, being so fearfully and wonderfully made, the overlapping of our physical and mental life is hard to untangle, it is important for Christians to remember that we are called to self-control in *all* seasons. The will of God for us, through physical and mental trials, is our sanctification. It's important that we realize this so we can have a gracious disposition in our communication toward our husband during these seasons. Just because you haven't gotten much sleep this month doesn't mean you get to treat him like an annoyance that you wish would disappear. Would you want him to treat you the same way when his work is hard?

So, if these hormones are real and genuinely influence how we perceive reality, why can't we let them call the shots? Well, it's precisely because they are a *skewed* perception of reality. They are telling only *part* of the story. To put it simply, it flat out isn't *true* that your husband doesn't love you because he *gets* to go to work every day while you care for the colicky baby. It may be true that your baby *is* fussier than the average baby and that you're genuinely lacking sleep, but it's likely a very short season and your husband does indeed love you or he wouldn't get up and walk out the door for work every morning, just as tired as you are. It's not *true* that you will be overwhelmed for the rest of forever because you haven't seen the bottom of the laundry pile in 8.6 months. It may be true that you are in an intense season of work in the home and very rarely get caught up on things, but it's because God has given you many blessings, and responsibilities require much heavy lifting. It's also true that you will likely adjust to the workload (if you keep your chin up), or that the Lord will meet your needs in a new way, including growing in contentment with so much work. Since difficulty does not automatically mean danger, and Christians are always safe because nothing can ultimately separate us from Christ, then we don't have to turn these difficulties into enemies, but rather see them as the very means that God intends to use to increase our faith and trust in Him.

In order to realign ourselves with truth so that we can most effectively communicate in these volatile times, it's highly important that we are in Scripture regularly. Scripture acts an anchor to us in the storms of life, stabilizing us and keeping us from drifting onto the shoals of falsehood and emotionalism. They remind us that Christ is holding us firm. Again, this doesn't mean we aren't really *feeling* a certain way, but that the Scriptures help us discern when our emotions don't genuinely represent reality.

One real-life example you may be familiar with is the intensity of newborn life, sleeplessness, and the emotions that come with it. Add something like norovirus or mastitis on top of it and you're toast! This isn't to shame you, but to reveal some of the traps we set for ourselves. You may be extremely tempted in seasons like this to forego Bible reading altogether. You're sick to your stomach, exhausted, and you *feel* like all you can manage to do is scroll social media while nursing the baby. You scroll, scroll, scroll, leaving imprints of images of gorgeous homes and overflowing gardens and happy children for your brain to meditate on in the middle of the night. You get frustrated that your current circumstances don't match up. The toddler wakes the finally sleeping baby a little earlier than you would have liked in the morning, and you're already annoyed that nothing is living up to the expectations you've suddenly placed on yourself overnight. You scream at the children and get out of fellowship way too fast, making your stomachache or infection worse in the meantime.

Instead, the habit you should have been cultivating, even when you *felt* too tired, is to go to Scripture. You can pick up a Bible and flip to a short Psalm just as easily as you can

pass your finger across your phone screen. Even more helpful may be just lying and listening to God's Word while you
cuddle a yummy-smelling newborn. You feel tired, and you
are tired, but it's untrue that you can't read the Bible. Truth
would have provided the vital meat necessary for the very
hard, very good task of caring for a newborn. It would have
given new perspective to the situation. It would have helped
you see that occasionally meddlesome toddler not as a nui-
sance, but as a *person*—a person so excited and thankful for
his new baby sibling that he couldn't wait to rush in and see
her in the morning, even though it woke her up early. See
how God's truth is an anchor when our big emotions want
to lead us astray?

Sometimes simply understanding how my body works
physically is in and of itself a protection to help me better
communicate with my husband. I might say something
like, "I know I shouldn't be anxious about this situation at
church, but I haven't been sleeping well with all the kids
being sick, and I just want you to know how I'm feeling right
now. Can you help me get my emotions in check?" Often
my husband can dispel my yuck feelings and put me back on
the right mental track with just a few sentences. I like plain
talk. It's easy to remember in the foggy depths of mother-
hood. I don't need flowery empathy; just a short statement
to reorient my bad attitude. Something said simply with a
smile, like, "That's silly and untrue. Don't believe that!" is
a genuine help to me. It's far easier to remember than an
elaborate five-point argument about why I shouldn't feel
the way I do when I'm running on five cups of coffee and
one hour of sleep.

During other times, I may have to admit my personal

responsibility for sinning. An example, considering the above situation with a toddler who wakes his sleeping newborn sibling, may look like, "I'm sorry, child. Mommy is very tired, but it was wrong for me to yell at you like that. I'm going to ask the Lord for forgiveness and help when I feel so tired, and I'd like to ask for your forgiveness as well." Again, don't allow your emotions to get you off the hook of being a responsible human being before the Lord. Having a predisposition toward a sin just means we should be even more watchful in physically trying times.

Some of you have genuinely been sinned against by your spouse, and that sin comes with very real emotions. Sin really does create discord and distance in marriages. Maybe you have genuinely been abandoned or made to feel less than because of abuse, adultery, or general lack of being cherished. First off, in these circumstances I would encourage you to go to a trusted elder and seek counsel in how to be reconciled in your marriage. Some marriage tangles can be complex and painful, and require outside hands to help untie. Even in ideal circumstances, where both spouses want to be reconciled and are willing to undertake the required work, there will still be challenging communication hurdles to jump over. But don't consider them too far gone for the Lord to be able to help you overcome.

In these circumstances, it will be very important to not rehearse the sins committed against you in your mind. This is quite literally how you plant bitterness: going down the row, plopping a tiny seed into each hole. Row by row, day by day, you water and tend to the seeds you've planted, and one day a giant, thorny, ugly weed pushes itself to the surface. This can be avoided by creating some new thought habits with God's help. Instead of meditating on the past sins of your spouse, tell yourself, "I will not keep a record of wrongs. Love believes all things (1 Cor. 13:7), and that includes that my spouse is a new creation in Christ (2 Cor. 5:16–17)."

If your spouse is a Christian, the reality is that Christ took the brutal consequences for the sins committed against you on the cross. You must forgive seven times seventy-seven. My husband pointed out to me recently that part of why Jesus tells the disciples to forgive in that manner is that some people and some situations do require indefinite amounts of forgiveness. I understand that trust often takes time to rebuild, and any reasonable spouse would be willing to understand that as well, but if your communication includes constantly throwing your husband's sin in his face, it would be right for him to point you to his Advocate, Jesus. "Take it up with him, honey. You said you've forgiven me, and it is no longer profitable to bring it up in this manner." This would be reasonable of your husband to say and do. I use the word *reasonable* a few times here, because our emotions are quick to make us *un*reasonable humans, but remember that God, in His kindness, gave us brains that know how to do logic, so use your brain. It is hard truths like this that we often need to run up against when our emotions are out of control.

My last bit of advice on reining in big emotions is to literally sing a Psalm. Before my husband made music for the public, he would often record Psalms and send them to me. Sometimes it was just for fun to see what I thought, but often the Lord used those Psalms to help me through trials. It has been such a blessing to hear how God's truth, recorded through my husband's music, has also gone out

to the entire Christian church and has been an encouragement to others through many trials: stillbirths, the death of
spouses, loss of children, or even just your garden-variety,
everyday struggles to be faithful.

I think this is precisely why Scripture encourages us to
sing to one another in Psalms. Singing truth seems to get
my heart back into the right disposition faster than almost
anything else can. God made our bodies with an intricacy
and brilliance that we have not even truly begun to appre-
ciate—and singing is just one example. Isn't it amazing that
God tuned our bodies and minds, tuning us in such a way
as to respond to certain wavelengths and patterns of sound
with calm, joy, sadness, and all the rest? Singing can literally vibrate certain muscles and nerves in ways that interact
with your nervous system and calm your entire body. I have
the Psalms playing to keep up morale on good days, but if
I need them on the good days, you can bet we have them
playing on the hard days just as much, if not more.

Now obviously, it's not all in the mere sounds; the content matters too. That's the reason I said to sing a *Psalm*.
The Psalms seem to uniquely deal with just about the whole
spectrum of human emotions. This is comforting to me,
because it shows me that God will not cast me out if I *feel*
something I shouldn't feel. David could go to Him with
depression, feelings of betrayal, fear for his safety, etc. Some
of David's big emotions were even the result of his very
own sins! He probably felt quite ashamed of himself when
he went to the Lord after committing adultery with Bath-
sheba. If David can find help from God amid such messy
circumstances, then you certainly can too.

CHAPTER 4

ON ANGER AND MANIPULATION

It's important for women to be aware that we are too often experts at trying to manipulate people with our emotions. This does not mean that every single time we feel sad or like we need something from our husbands we are manipulating him, but it is good for us to be aware that we are prone to this temptation.

Some women manipulate with tears. Others manipulate by giving the cold shoulder or withholding sex. And still others may try to manipulate their way into a better marriage by spending a lot of the time angry. As a Christian, this last one often feels very easy to justify in our minds—especially when real sin is involved—because it makes us feel holy. We think, "We should be angry at things that anger God!" We need to understand that prolonged anger is not a tool that God gives us permission to use in our marriages. This is why Ephesians 4:26 tells us to not even let the sun go down on our anger. No, this does *not* mean you must

stay up until 4 a.m. to complete the conversation and get
to a resolution. We are also humans, and sometimes getting
some sleep will put out the fiery emotions in a way that
makes finishing the conversation the next day much more
productive. What it often means in these kinds of situations
is that your *anger* needs to simply be put to bed, followed by
yourself, with the intention of calmly and fruitfully working
through whatever issue remains unresolved the next day.

James 1:20 tell us that "the anger of man does not pro-
duce the righteousness of God." Think about it: Jesus didn't
cast a stern look our way and thus turn us into new cre-
ations. Instead, He laid His actual life down for us so we
could be reconciled to Him. Why in the world do we as
women think that outbursts of wrath, swearing, and cutting
down our husband in front of the children will bring rec-
onciliation in the long run? It is painful to deny ourselves
these reactions, but being sanctified often feels like cruci-
fixion. Scripture is clear that it's the quiet and gentle spirit
of wives that wins disobedient husbands over to obedience
(1 Pet. 3:1–4), not the angry and harsh spirit, the nagging
and rude spirit, or the combative and controlling spirit.

One of my children was making a fuss over something
absolutely silly the other day. I was chuckling at him while
watching from across the room. After a moment of watching
him in his frustration, I asked him the same thing God asked
Jonah when Jonah was annoyed with the plant: "Do you do
well to be angry?" (Jonah 4:9). My child was startled, looked
around for a moment, and then proceeded to laugh at himself. Sometimes we really do need to ask ourselves that same
question. Maybe your husband really does fail to get home
on time most nights of the week. Maybe he is forgetful about

birthdays and special holidays. Maybe he has overlooked the fact that perhaps you could use a night out at a quiet bookstore alone. But do you do well to be *angry* about it?

Hosea 11:4 says, "I led them with cords of kindness, with the bands of love, and I became to them as one who eases the yoke on their jaws, and I bent down to them and fed them." This verse reminds me so much of my husband anytime I read it. He is not a man who is quick to anger and never has been. He is patient and so charitable, even toward his enemies. When I feel tempted to be angry about any situation in life, even beyond marriage, I often think about how my husband mimics the Lord to me by drawing me in with cords of kindness, even when I'm being an undeserving twerp. I've seen him time and time again return harsh criticism with a smile and a nod and let it roll off his back. It really has been shocking to watch as an adult, but I'm so thankful for the example it has set for me because it enabled me to see that there genuinely are other legitimate responses to circumstances that aren't the greatest. You don't *have* to be angry on autopilot. Some people really didn't grow up with positive examples, and they need to realize that they are responsible to set new standards of behavior in their homes and marriages.

As my little boys are turning into young men before my very eyes, I am learning just how true it is that a soft answer turns away wrath (Prov. 15:1). I want to communicate my respect to them as they grow into their own well-informed opinions and become the men God has made them to be. When we differ, I see how quickly I can stoke the flames of frustration with a thoughtless critique. The flip side of this verse is that providing a soft answer for a frustrated response can quickly put out the fire that was being stoked to dangerous levels. Many times, I can physically see a conversation starting to escalate and when I pray for grace and get self-control of my tongue, I am able to absorb the provocation without needing to provoke in return.

The same thing is possible in marriage. Just because your husband had a hard day at work and is maybe being too short with you and the kids doesn't mean that returning in kind will be the solution. Yes, husbands sin. What will you do with it? How will you respond? Why not ask a question that shows you care about his day not going well and you want to help so he doesn't feel so frustrated? "It seems like the meeting didn't go so well. I'm sorry. Do you want to go for a run alone after dinner?"

My last thought is a sobering reminder that being angry is often a pure waste of time. When it comes to anger, my husband often reminds the congregation that even righteous anger must be quickly turned to righteous action, lest it curdle into sin and bitterness. Anger that isn't quickly turned to righteous action—even if that action is simply prayerfully entrusting the anger to the Lord—isn't constructive. Let's be honest with ourselves: It almost always makes everything worse. What does the angry person need? Wisdom to know how to act righteously in hard circumstances. This is a great case for learning how to plead with God for wisdom (James 1:5). Thankfully, that is a prayer He *loves* to answer.

CHAPTER 5

GET OUT YOUR OVEN MITTS

Modern therapy wants us to get real cozy with our emotions. Therapists want us to analyze our emotions with a magnifying glass, dissect them, give them pet names, and occasionally, release them if they *don't serve us well*. For some emotions we have pills. Others come with drastic lifestyle changes—ranging from the forcible removal of all "toxic" people from our lives to the investment of 3.7 days a week in meditation to balance our chakras.

There are many problems with this approach, but the main issue we will deal with in this chapter is that we ought to understand that spending too much time in the boggy water of our emotional wellbeing *simply isn't safe*. Staring more and more deeply into your own navel just isn't a good idea; you won't find wellsprings of truth, goodness, and beauty there. Emotional self-discovery and endless emotional self-analysis aren't the answer to our problems. Some emotions don't need to be immediately and endlessly analyzed, but rather handled with oven mitts and held out at arm's length. Like a hot-out-of-the-oven apple pie that needs to be set aside to cool down a bit, so do some emotions. Get some distance from your emotions. Give yourself the space and time to approach your feelings with clarity and care, rather than acting on them impulsively or spilling them onto others.

Here is an example of an emotion that isn't safe to hang out with. As I mentioned in the last chapter, my husband is fond of saying that anger is swift to curdle. The Bible instructs us to be angry and not sin, which means it must be possible to be righteously angry, but we can't overlook the plain fact that it means it's *also* possible to sin in our anger. It may be true that your husband has been thoughtless about how much housework you have to do and you could really use a few extra hands after the kids' bedtime to tidy up at night, but it's not going to help if you let that anger curdle into a sour attitude of distance and iciness toward your husband. You can *really* be sinned against and *really* sin in return. This is how a marriage goes sour in a hurry.

Our culture has catechized us to believe that every single thing we feel is just, valid, and worthy of exploration. "I am right to be grumpy at the kids, because I spent all day mopping yesterday and they spilled syrup all over the kitchen floor this morning! Nobody appreciates my hard work!" Some people are genuinely hoodwinked into believing their feelings are unqualified reality. "You *are* a hurtful husband, because you called me out on the way I rolled my eyes, but you didn't even stop to ask *why* I rolled my eyes! It was because you hurt my feelings when you came home 15 minutes late from work! You don't even want to be with me." In this interpretation, her husband really *is* the jerk and she really *is* the victim of his tardy-from-work jerkiness. But is it true? No. In reality, *she* was being the disrespectful jerk to her husband, and he was correct to call her out. He was doing his duty, actually (Eph. 5:26–27). In fact, *she* really owes *him* an apology.

Once, in the depths of life with a fourth newborn, I remember 1 Peter 4:1–2 being a specific help to me. It says, "Since therefore Christ suffered in the flesh, arm yourselves with the same way of thinking, for whoever has suffered in the flesh has ceased from sin, so as to live for the rest of the time in the flesh *no longer for human passions but for the will of God.*" After many easy pregnancies, labors, and newborns, baby number four felt like a doozy to me. In reality, I needed to lower some of my standards so I could increase the *right* standards. I remember sharing my feelings with a friend and identifying with what she said when she was in a similar position: "I knew I was in a sticky place when I was jealous of my husband who left to work at a construction site each day!" Thankfully, we laughed together and then she encouraged me to keep plodding in my mothering. But the verse in 1 Peter 4 showed me that Christ's suffering, death, and resurrection had made it possible for me to arm myself with a way of thinking that equipped me to live *against* my human passions—against my *feelings*. I didn't *have* to give in to the feeling of mental and physical exhaustion, decision fatigue, and resentment. Sure, I probably needed to take more naps than usual, but I needed to remember that my *feelings* didn't have to control my thoughts. In fact, I had the very mind of Christ that would enable me to triumph over these self-indulgent patterns of thinking.

Oversharing is another symptom of this emotional self-obsession that I see women indulging themselves in. Social media has definitely added to this problem, as well as a false understanding of what it means to be authentic. Proverbs 12:16[1] teaches us the principle that immediate sharing of emotions, particularly the emotion of *vexation*, is often the behavior of the fool. As a matter of fact, many places in Scripture, including this one in Proverbs, show us how glorious it is to be able to overlook some hurts entirely. Instead of going to the ear of another sister and sharing every grief you have with your husband from the last seventy-two hours, get on your knees in your prayer closet. The Lord is the only one with the jurisdiction to help in every single situation, after all. Going to your sisters in Christ often puts them in an awkward position; they may have to eventually ask you to stop sharing when it crosses the line or affects how they view your husband. The faster I can go to the Lord with my most concerning worries, the stronger that muscle becomes of being able to trust Him to care for me and not take matters into my own hands. His grace really does prove sufficient to help us overlook annoyances, big and little, and as we bring those things to him, we really do grow in Christlike qualities.

After you spend a good amount of time being suspicious of your own emotions and asking the Lord to help you wade through them safely and wisely, you will be more equipped to discuss them with your husband fruitfully. You will be able to sort through them more accurately, discerning the ones you need help with. But often you will find that you

---

1. Proverbs 12:16 reads, "The vexation of a fool is known at once, but the prudent ignores an insult."

don't even need to "work through" many of these feelings, but rather cast them on the Lord and move on with grace and not bitterness. I am not saying that you should stifle your feelings in an inhuman way—we are not robots, and our emotions are good gifts from our Father—but rather, I encourage you to know that the only place they are perfectly safe is with the Lord, since he alone is able to keep account of your sorrows and tears (Ps. 56:8).

CHAPTER 6

RESPECT

The table is beautifully landscaped for a friendly Sabbath meal. The linen tablecloth is ironed just so. The colorful crystal glasses are filled with chilled sweet tea, the texture of the chargers offset perfectly by the porcelain plates. The inviting smell of deliciously tender meat mingles with the vanilla cake that's cooling in the kitchen. Drinks and conversation are enjoyed while the hostess pulls together the final details for the meal. But nobody is prepared for the bad attitude that is about to send a jarring, discordant note clanging through the harmony of fellowship. It didn't take much to bring the warm and inviting scene to a grating halt—just one sour comment shot rudely from wife to husband.

We've all been there. I've been in many awkward situations as a pastor's wife, but these situations are still the ones that leave me feeling confused and downright put off. What does the husband do now? Address it then and there? Maybe. Would it feel shameful to her? Highly likely. Does someone else call her out? Everyone saw it happen.

Everyone feels awkward for themselves and even worse for the husband. Most often, everyone tries his best to push through the awkwardness and get back to normalcy, but the bad note still rings in the air even so.

How do we prevent this kind of thing? Before I answer, consider a question: When is the last time you heard a sermon specifically rebuking disrespectful speech in women that didn't offer a few dozen qualifications—and especially one that didn't immediately try to pin some significant portion of the blame for rude and disrespectful women on their husbands? Pretty rare, isn't it? Why is that? Why would that be so rare given that it is *not* a rarity for Scripture to address these exact sins common to women and their corresponding virtues? For examples, just read Proverbs 14:1; 19:13; 21:9, 19; 25:24; 27:15–16; 31:26–28; 1 Peter 3:1–4; and Titus 2:3–5.

So how do we prevent women from walking in unrepentantly disrespectful speech, particularly to their husbands? We probably have to talk about it more directly and clearly; to *name* the sin. And so, one of the best ways to head off these unnecessary interruptions to fellowship is to simply and cheerfully teach our women the standard of respectful speech to their own husbands. This needs to be done with gentleness, but also with directness, bringing clear correction when a habit of disrespectful speech rears its head.

Obviously, husbands have a great deal of responsibility for the behavior of their wives and should feel free to bring needed correction concerning this issue, but I do think this is a very important place for mature, godly women to speak into one another's lives. I can still remember the day a gray-haired lady pulled me aside at church to gently correct me for some polite poking that I did to my fiancé in a public conversation. I was nineteen at the time and the conversation was blunt and helpful.

"Never correct your husband in front of others unless it is of genuine spiritual and eternal importance. You are his public relations manager."

I knew this woman was married to a difficult man. Her words meant even more to me because I had witnessed her on many occasions walk the walk of being a kind and respectful wife to her husband, overlooking many instances where discretion and grace were lacking almost entirely in her husband. The edifying exchange never led to feelings of ongoing frustration with this older sister, but rather I respected her and knew that she respected her husband and my future husband.

With so few examples of godly and applied femininity in marriages today, I think a lot of women simply don't know what respect actually looks like. My experience has been largely positive in bringing clear and gentle correction to younger women; on the fairly rare occasions I have needed to point these things out to sisters in my circles, they have generally repented and changed their behavior quickly. This is especially true in women who are otherwise godly and seeking to please the Lord—they often simply aren't aware of the issue. It is invisible to them. I know sometimes I personally need the simple and small correction of, "Not this way, but this way," and then I can make greater strides toward Christlike character. For some, it really is a simple renewing of the mind; a one-time changing of a sticking thought pattern.

Here are a few habits to consider in your speech toward

your husband that, once made apparent to you, will click into place in no time with simple practice:

Do not interrupt your husband. Don't do it when he's telling a story to friends, when it's just your family at the dinner table, in front of new people, or telling his brothers a story. Interrupting is almost always disrespectful and rude behavior in any case, so how much more in a relationship where God specifically commands you to show particular respect? If interrupting is a habit, make a practice of pausing for a few beats after someone speaks before you jump in. If you're always waiting for the slightest intake of breath to start talking, you simply will develop a habit of interrupting.

Make it a habit to let small details go uncorrected. It is extremely unbecoming of a woman to be so fastidious about facts that she feels the need to offer live "fact-checking" of her husband's words in the moment as he tells an anecdote or discusses some event or other. Consider how you would feel if things were reversed—usually hurt, embarrassed, or at the least, annoyed. A husband doesn't want to have to steer the conversational ship back to his intended destination just because you had some interesting side note you felt compelled to add or some correction to make.

Make sure you are giving him room to speak, too. I think it's important for women to learn to not be conversation hogs. I know some personalities in marriages are genuinely more talkative than others. This is good and fitting for some folks and certain dispositions. But there is a difference between a woman who talks a lot because she has a habit of steamrolling her husband—never letting him get a word in edgewise—and a woman who talks a lot because her husband is quieter by disposition and genuinely happy to let her talk more. You know it when you see it, and be honest: You don't like it when you see it in others, do you?

Don't settle into a pattern of regular snark and sarcasm. This is a massive temptation for women today; I think it is one of the chief culprits in dysfunctional and disrespectful speech from wives to their husbands. Our feminist-saturated culture is partly to blame for the spillover of this mode of communication into the church today. Feminists are always trying to convince godly women to compete for a place with the men. I think of snark and sarcasm as wartime communication, basically verbal pugilism, and women ought not have anything to do with the battlefield. Think about it: Snark and sarcasm are cutting things. They are weapons you use to destroy an enemy or cut down an opponent. Is your husband your enemy? Is he your opponent? Would you deploy cutting sarcasm in speaking to the Lord? If not, why would you take it up in speaking to your lowercase-l lord (1 Pet. 3:6)? These are tools in the communication tool belt that women simply ought to throw away in most circumstances. Refuse to give in to the peer pressure and social engineering of feminism. The woman who constantly turns to the weaponry of biting sarcasm is trying to be one of the guys. Instead, we need to learn to speak like ladies.

Women who have a disposition toward sarcasm and snarkiness are often women who have genuinely been gifted with brilliant minds. They are smart and want to outwit their opponents—but again, what happens when the opponent she finds herself sparring with is her own husband? As women, Scripture is clear that we aren't to win others over with biting wit and dazzling displays of cutting rhetoric.

In Scripture, women are urged to win others over with a quiet, gentle spirit and good works. No need to add a dash of sass into the mix. But often, women with these gifts have a hard time putting down something that feels so shiny and impressive in their own minds. Now, I'm not saying that women with impressive gifts of intellect need to play dumb or neglect the cultivation of these gifts—after all, like all good gifts, the gift of a ready mind was given by God. But these women need to channel all that intellectual energy into the good works God has appointed. The opportunities are nearly endless on this front! She can throw herself into the pursuit of knowledge that results in care of husbands and homes and children, knowledge that leads to flourishing churches, information that doesn't just stop in an idealistic realm, but gives birth to culture, to tasty meals, to robust vocations. She can ponder the mysteries of the faith, study the Scriptures, and pursue countless avenues of learning and interest. But none of this requires her to take up the sword of unladylike verbal pugilism, particularly the kind directed at her own people.

One possible solution to this problem is that when you are tempted to dish out a snarky comment, pray in your heart and ask the Lord to show you a reason to be thankful for your husband instead. When I do this, it often shows me how unreasonable and rude I'm being and helps me get my feet back on the path of respectful conduct toward my man. Another solution for when you're really feeling bothered is to simply hold your tongue. Again, it is good for women to practice being *quiet*. The fool's vexation is known at once, but it's to your glory to overlook the annoyance.

Believe me, there are times when I find myself thinking

I know a thing or two more than the man God has given to lead me. In these moments, my flesh wants nothing more than to find a way to justify the snarky and disrespectful speech I'm tempted to let fly. I know our culture would find the principles I just gave to be shockingly offensive—but then I remember that it is actually our androgynous and rampantly disrespectful *culture* that is shocking, not these simple principles. In His kindness, the Lord has helped me see that I really don't need to say half as much as I think I do. Everyone is the better for me keeping sinfully snarky and sarcastic comments to myself, especially me.

CHAPTER 7

ON BEING LOW MAINTENANCE

I want to be a woman who can eat and fish and carry two buckets.

— NANCY WILSON

When someone says, "Oh, they're high maintenance!" I'm sure many of us imagine a buxom blonde sitting in a swivel chair at a hair salon while being doted upon. One servant paints her toenails while another gives her a manicure, another rubs her shoulders, and yet another curls her hair. She's probably wearing the most recent styles from Nordstrom, complete with a matching handbag with a tiny animal tucked inside.

The older I get, the more I realize that there is a much more common, much more garden-variety version of the high-maintenance woman who doesn't resemble this caricature at all. Because it's tricky to spot, I think it can sometimes be hard for women to see how they are being high maintenance. More importantly, these women may not understand why they need to lay down some of their wants and desires so they can instead receive the life, vocation, and identity that God is giving to them.

What do I mean by this? The high-maintenance woman is the woman who clings much too tightly and unreasonably to a desire—spoken or (often) unspoken—that she feels she deserves. At the hint of a threat to this desire, she will begin to spiral into anxiety, fussing, or anger. A new mom may desire her husband's physical presence in person or his attention via texts and phone calls when he's away too much, keeping him from his own workload and duties. Another woman may be much too emotionally needy, unwilling to take responsibility for her own sin and emotions, and instead expecting everyone around her to be an on-demand listening ear. She is not, as Paul urges, carrying her own load (Gal. 6:5), but demanding everyone else carry it for her.

One woman may bring into marriage the unspoken desire of a five-bedroom house with a three-car garage right up the street from her sister, who is also her best friend. This isn't necessarily a wrong or disordered desire—extended family is a true blessing, as is a nice house. But if she's hanging all her longing and directing all the details of her life toward this one, specific desire, then descending into fury when her husband gets promoted, which necessitates a move two states over, she has missed the mark. Her life goals were not properly aligned with the Lord's goals for her, so now she's going to be fussy and make her husband's life a low-grade thunderstorm in the background for the foreseeable future. Not only that, but she's also likely to overlook the hard work he has done to get that promotion, enabling them to get a bigger house, even if it's in a different location. High-maintenance desires should never get in the way of the goals the Lord and our husbands have set for our families.

I have heard many a faithful pastor remind men and women that the woman is not the mission of marriage. Not even the husband is free to make the woman the mission of marriage. Rather, she is his helper in pursuing the mission God has entrusted the home: God's glory, furthering His church through our homes and families. This sort of mission requires adaptability, flexibility, fearlessness, and courage from women. I believe this is precisely why Scripture calls us to imitate our mother in the faith, Sarah, and to not fear anything that is fearful (1 Pet. 3:1–6). High-maintenance desires often get in the way of cultivating these godly feminine traits, because they make us fragile when things don't go our way—and as hard as it may be to hear, things often won't go our way in this life. This is actually a part of God's kindness toward us, as He works all things together for our good (Rom. 8:28).

What am I urging you to be and do? Let me state it plainly: *Be a wife who is easy to please.* Let me take a moment and explain why this is a worthy goal.

Our husbands are more effective when they don't have to carry their own work and emotional load in addition to ours. Part of being low maintenance is not needing to be babysat or micromanaged in the home. My husband often says wives should be their husbands' chief deputies. As women, we have genuine authority to make decisions, direct people, and use resources wisely in our domains. If you constantly feel like you want your husband to check in with you daily or weekly, consider the fact that what you need may not be an extra word of encouragement, but simply a little more maturity to be humble enough to do hidden work that nobody sees, including your husband.

There are genuine seasons in which I need my husband to watch me work, look over my lists, and give input and direction. I try to make these times few and far between because I know part of my job during the day is keeping the house and family running in such a way that he can come home and find fellowship, rest, and refreshment, and not another project he has to do. It's not that your husband doesn't love you if he isn't constantly interested in the details of domestic life. It's that he loves you so much that he needs and wants to be able to do his work well so he can continue to provide for you. Could you imagine if your banker husband came home with a briefcase full of accounts he needed you to settle for him? This is a double standard that women hold where they expect a lot more help in the home from their husbands than they really should need, all the while completely understanding how unreasonable it would be if the roles were reversed.

Being easy to please often accompanies being easy to find things to be thankful for. Scripture is clear that the tongue is a powerful tool for life and death (Prov. 18:21). A woman who is quick to use her tongue to find things to praise in others and in hard circumstances is a low-maintenance woman. A thankful woman is an anti-fragile woman. The Christian life requires much self-denial and many unexpected and unwanted turns, but a low-maintenance woman understands that every struggle that happens to her, to her marriage, and to her family is a gift straight from the hand of God. With author Elisabeth Elliot, low-maintenance women can say, "Leave it all in the hands that were pierced for you!"

It may seem counterintuitive, but I think low-maintenance women are women who voice their desires and wants simply and directly. They are not willing to hide unspoken requests from others, using their ever-shifting desires to manipulate people and situations. Low-maintenance people have gone through the mental work of figuring out what their true needs are, then humbly and cheerfully asking for them. This doesn't mean she is constantly demanding everyone around her fulfill her every whim and petty desire—on the contrary, the habit of clear and consistent verbalization of her desires helps her guard against being overly needy. Saying things out loud has an accountability of its own. She is being courteous enough to her husband and to others to make herself plainly understood, rather than operating by hints, whispers, and manipulation tactics.

One example of this may be a wife realizing there is some tool she needs to make her work around the house more effective. It may be a new vacuum that has special attachments for the different types of flooring in their home. She thinks it's the perfect device to enable the kids to help out more, thus freeing her up for other work. If she's a high-maintenance woman who buys endless gadgets, thinking they will take the work out of her workload at home—failing to realize that what the home really needs is for her to simply show up and apply herself a little more often, even when she doesn't *feel* like it—then her husband may sigh and give in and buy yet another gadget. On the other hand, he may be frustrated and deny her request altogether.

But if she's a wife who works hard, often makes do with what she has, is a creative problem solver and doesn't complain in her husband's ears or ask him to pick up her slack regularly, then he will consider her request and likely grant her desire within reason. Her husband trusts she will use his money toward effective and fruitful ends in his home because he knows she works with willing hands. He knows she's been cheerful in lean seasons and that she genuinely tries her hardest. She isn't abdicating her work to him or the children. Because she has regularly proven herself to be a woman who can carry a heavy load cheerfully, he is inclined to help her out however she needs when she does make a wise request.

Early in my marriage and parenting, I was grateful for a few wiser, older women God brought across my path. I learned many helpful, godly traits from them, and I know they also left similar impressions on many other young women around me. Some of the traits common to all these women were that they regularly had a smile on their faces and worked with willing hands that were adaptable at a moment's notice. Their eyes and minds were on the hunt for thoughtful ways to help others around them. Their homes overflowed with hospitality, and they were easy conversationalists who always had something to share that they were thankful for or an interesting book they were reading. Good works literally overflowed their hearts, lips, fingertips, and tables. Their very persons were adorned with the kind of Christian virtue that shines as an unfading glory. These traits mark them as some of the most feminine women I've met in my life. These women have also been some of the most low-maintenance people I've ever met.

Let the reader understand.

CHAPTER 8

GROW UP

Over the years, I have heard about some very silly things married couples choose to fight about. Occasionally in the course of counseling couples through some difficulty or other, my husband would ask me to speak with the wife. One of the things we quickly learned was how much time and resources are wasted simply because spouses are not mature enough to know when to pick or not pick a fight. A lot of women need the simple exhortation: "This is not a hill to die on. Move along, Sis!"

A real-life example will be helpful to see what I mean.[1] When I was a few days postpartum with our second child, my husband got a frantic phone call from a new husband in the church. They needed to meet *as soon as possible*. It was in the evening, and we had just clipped our toddler into his booster seat at the table to feed him some dinner. My husband was helping our son while I nursed the newborn. We didn't typically take on extra ministry work in the first few

---

1. Some of the details are changed in this example for the sake of privacy.

weeks after a birth, but the husband said this was serious and they needed help.

As is often the case with these situations, I try to help as much as I can, while my real job is to keep the kids happy and limit their interruptions or distractions. I laid the newborn back down, left my husband to lead the conversation, but soon returned to take over feeding our oldest. As two-year-olds do, he found the adult conversation quite boring and started waddling around our tiny living room with his dinner seat still attached. I didn't want to cause a scene, so I let our son waddle around while I snuck a bite or two into his mouth here and there.

I watched my husband's confused face as he kept listening for the big sin that he was to counsel and chastise the husband for. It was clear that the wife was quite worked up, gesticulating wildly and listing out the many annoyances that had been bothering her since their return home from their honeymoon. Fairly early in the conversation, our newborn began to cry just as I awkwardly got the toddler back to the table to sit down. The fussy dinnertime hour was obviously upon us and our littlest guy didn't want to be consoled, no matter what I tried.

Unaware of how much of an inconvenience this couple was being to a very tired family, the wife looked at me with an extremely frazzled expression as I tried everything to calm the newborn. I was obnoxiously bouncing him around our tiny 700-square-foot condo in a vain attempt to get him to go to sleep when she finally said, "CAN YOU GET HIM TO BE QUIET!?"

Stunned, my husband quickly intervened and brought the conversation to the point: "Just what is it that you guys are here for and need counsel about?"

Quickly, the wife voiced the main complaint and reason for their immediate need for help: "Well, you see, he didn't take the trash out when he *said* he did!"

My husband laughed.

"That's it? Nothing else?"

"Yeah! That's it! He lied and it really hurt me!"

Now even more confused, my husband responded again. "Are you sure there's nothing else causing all this uproar?" He hesitated and then asked the husband, "You didn't look at porn or do something more than the trash-taking-out lie?"

The husband shook his head.

I don't remember how my husband wrapped up the very impromptu counseling session, but since then we've had to learn that we can't be the 911 emergency solution to all marriage problems for couples. But it's astonishing just how often this theme—drag-out fights surrounding very minor and silly themes—has recurred in the midst of counseling and mentoring men and women in their marriages. One thing that just about always lives at the root of issues like this? A simple lack of maturity.

Maturity helps you know when something is worth putting your foot down over and planting a flag. For a wife, this needs to be over a genuine sin issue she sees in her husband, not simply a certain habit or character trait she wished her husband had or didn't have. *"All* really godly husbands *lift weights"* is a ridiculous thing to fight about in your marriage. Rather, confronting your husband because you found out he's been looking at porn is something worth discussing.

We sometimes persist in immature fights *knowing* we are being immature because we are measuring how much our spouse loves us by the amount of stink eye they are willing to put up with. It's a yucky, underhanded way to test your spouse's faithfulness. To this behavior Paul would encourage you to be mature in your thinking (1 Cor. 14:20). We genuinely act like toddlers when we do this sort of thing; toddlers will throw fits to make sure their parents do love and discipline them. Toddler tactics aren't helpful marriage tactics. We want to bring up *real* concerns, overlooking as much as we can, so that we have the energy and resources needed to help solve *real* problems.

Let me share some examples of immature fights to help you see if you are doing this in your marriage. It's usually never okay to fight over your spouse putting the toilet paper on the holder the wrong way, the fact that the dinner you made wasn't his favorite, his failure to comment on how dainty your new pair of shoes makes your feet look, who does the dinner dishes, or who has the correct song lyrics memorized and who doesn't. Several of these are issues my husband and I have silent agreements never to fight over. We can poke a little fun at each other and move on quickly, knowing very well that some things just aren't worth arguing about. We have important goals to accomplish together—why waste time arguing over pointless minutia? We have no resources to waste over minor upsets in light of the vast mission God has entrusted to our household. Who cares how the toilet paper hangs when there are disciples to baptize, kids to catechize, and nations to convert? As a Christian, you have a lot of good work to get to—good work the Lord has put in front of your feet to walk in (Eph. 2:10). Most of these good works are mundane, ordinary tasks like doing the laundry so your kids have clean clothes for the week. One thing that will certainly keep you from walking faithfully in these good works? Letting yourself get constantly drunk on frustration and annoyance over what quite frankly amounts to stupid and insignificant issues.

Weekends and emotion-filled events like birthdays and holidays can present the biggest challenges. Be aware of this ahead of time. Many a family party has been ruined by an impatient comment and a returned nasty response. This ought not be the case. Instead, let's go into these big, life-marking events with a spirit of watchfulness, looking for the ways we may be tempted to slip up. Have a game plan in mind. Something like, "This holiday isn't about me. If none of the men offer to help with dishes, I won't be cold and grumpy all evening. I am here to serve freely as Christ has served me freely."

Will holidays and weekends magically be less tiring because you mastered your temper? It's not a guarantee, but the peace that comes from knowing your integrity is intact and God has helped you grow your spiritual muscles is a unique joy to be treasured. You will still be tired from your duties, just as your husband will if he is doing his, but you won't be exhausted from spending all your energy on meaningless fights with the very people you were called to love and serve.

If we're honest with ourselves, simple selfishness is at the root of many annoyances that turn into all-out brawls. James 4:1–2 tells us that we quarrel because we desire and do not have. We are often focused *only* on ourselves in these circumstances, which leads to grabby hands and grabby hearts. Those verses also tell us that part of why we don't have the things we desire is because we haven't asked the Lord for them. This must mean that it's actually okay to ask

God for the things we may be desiring, as long as we can meekly submit to His answer. Would you like a date night this month? Okay, pray about it and ask the Lord to provide. Has the month ended and your husband didn't initiate or plan anything for just the two of you? Then you know the Lord either wants you to be content without, get creative with at-home date nights, or He may want you to take responsibility for this yourself. But you can be certain at this point, after praying, that the Lord does *not* want you to pout about it until your husband magically learns to read your mind.

My last tidbit of advice is to cultivate the simple willingness to keep quiet and learn to overlook many small annoyances and inconveniences, even if you know or feel you really are justified in your feelings. The peace and unity of your marriage is more important than playing "fact-checker" or proving to your husband that he really is as stupid as you're trying to make him feel. Your marriage will make swifter strides forward as you channel your energy toward the mission God has called your family to, rather than scattering your strength across the battlefield of needless fighting.

CHAPTER 9

FAITHFUL ARE THE WOUNDS OF A FRIEND

"Well, I've figured out the solution. We simply can't go to the midweek church meeting in this season of life."

I remember the certainty I felt as I made this announcement to my husband on the way home from the midweek church meeting one fall night. We bumped across potholes on a road through our neighborhood as we passed the nearby graveyard. I even remember all the Christmas lights, because they lit up his face while I looked at him, smiling, awaiting his agreement. It was obvious to me that taking a child to the bathroom every 15 minutes was really cramping our social life, and it made *zero sense* in my mom brain to make the inconvenient trek to the meeting. It just wasn't efficient; therefore, we need not go.

"We most certainly *are* going to go back to the midweek church meeting next week and he's coming with us."

This was the first time in my memory that my husband and I were coming to a true cross in our parenting journey. In general, we have always gotten along well, and I *do* recommend you get along with your spouse. But, because we had gotten along so well, it felt excruciating hearing him cross my thoughts on this opinion. It felt like betrayal of a Shakespearean kind.

Go back!? How could he demand such nonsense of me!? Doesn't he know I simply walk in the door to head to the bathroom with this twerp all night?! Nobody even cares that I've been sitting in the bathroom all day at home!? Why would we leave the house if I just have to do the same thing at someone else's house? What's the point? I was too stunned by his correction to say any of this out loud, but my immaturity showed itself inside.

He was calling me out in such a way that showed I had my priorities out of alignment. It was a true cross my flesh didn't want to bear, because it required death to self. Part of that death to self was hearing my husband's correction. On top of my negative feelings about the church event, this correction felt like a fresh blow. Luckily, the Spirit quickly breathed a moment of truth into my selfishness.

"Faithful are the wounds of a friend. Faithful are the wounds of your husband. It feels like he's hurting you, but he's trying to help you."

I knew instantly what my marching orders were: Go back to the midweek gathering next week, with a potty-training toddler in tow, and do it cheerfully. I don't remember how the rest of the conversation went, but I know we stayed in fellowship and those weekly treks were a major training ground for me to figure out how to navigate regular church life with my children. God used it to show me that my husband's leadership was for my spiritual good, even when it felt like it was leading me toward death. In reality, he *was* leading me toward death, but it was a death to self that included resurrection, joy, and life on the other side. My husband knew me and my specific temptations. He could see that I needed to grow up out of my selfish attitudes in regard to my public life with my children. It wasn't simply a problem of efficiency as my flesh wanted to believe, but rather a problem of character. The problem wasn't *out there* in the world or our circumstances, but *in my own* heart and mind, which needed renewing.

Our husbands have a unique insight into our pet anxieties. It could be over where the kids will go to college, what your in-laws expect of you for the holidays, or what the other family in the pew next to you thinks about your decision to pull one of the kids out of school for the rest of the year. Our feelings often make us feel like it's *reasonable* to be anxious about such things and to make decisions accordingly. But Philippians is clear that because the Lord is always at hand, the *more* reasonable option is to *not* be anxious (Phil. 4:5–6). Our husbands have a duty to plainly point out these things to us when we need it. In doing so, they live out their God-given vocation of leadership, taking us into greener pastures. Their job requires them to lead the family on the mission God has laid out before each of us— and sometimes this means helping us keep our priorities in check and not get sidetracked by lesser things.

Let's stop here for a second. Yes, your husband should be patient, kind, and merciful when he's pointing something out to you, but there's no easy way to say a hard thing. If he's trying to show you where you're in sin, it just *is* going to feel awkward and clunky and sometimes offensive to our sensibilities. Feeling these things doesn't mean he's in sin, being mean to you, or being harsh. It's the nature of hard conversations that they are, well, *hard*. And because most of us don't actually love one another enough to do this anymore—to have hard conversations—it tends to make our skin crawl. What am I saying? Here's one thing: Cut him some slack and be grateful he isn't scared of you. As a matter of fact, tell him that. And if you haven't had conversations like this ever, maybe you need to consider approaching your husband and giving him permission to correct you when you need it. I promise, you don't want a husband who is scared of you. A husband scared to lead his wife in this way is a man lacking resolution. He is often not a man worth listening to or following.

This means you need to consider your disposition when such concerns are brought up. Has he or anyone ever come to you with something they see that needs correction? Was your reaction harsh? Or were you meek and humble? Did you say you would pray about what they said? Did you then actually pray about it? Or did you brush it off and consider their concerns unfounded? Were you defensive? Prickly? Did you stonewall or give them the silent treatment for the next week?

If you're thinking back and you've realized you haven't been the most gracious when it comes to receiving correction, there's a simple solution: Apologize without excuse and get the lines of communication open again. Don't wait until you *feel* like apologizing. Again, hard conversations like this rarely flow naturally. I actually find it easier to apologize right away before there's time for my emotions to talk me into justifying my behavior further and creating more distance in the relationship. When your husband sees that you are eager to be led in your spiritual journey, it will kindle in him patience and kindness toward you.

I was thinking the other day about the older women who have helped me the most in my faith, and I thought about all of their marriages. The one thing that stood out to me about each woman was how obvious it was to me from day one that they allowed their husbands to shape who they were. They were truly more shaped and led by their husbands than they were by the other women in their church, by their elders, by the books they read, or by any other influence in their life. It was a great reminder to me to not take lightly the advice or insights my husband offers me.

Women today make light of a man's opinion because there is an odd belief that a man simply can't speak to a woman's problems. They say we need specific and formal one-on-one *female*-led counseling. Many mainstream churches believe there even needs to be a female voice to represent the women in the church during elders' meetings.[1] As this line of thinking goes, there simply *must* be an official women's ministry, led by women who are teaching other women doctrine. How else will the women in the church

---

1. Many years ago, I was helping with a women's retreat with my husband. One of the speakers was Jen Wilkin, a popular female Bible teacher. At one point, we had a lengthy conversation with her in which she told my husband (a pastor) that he needed to immediately begin including me in the elders' meetings, lest the church fail to have a properly ordered female perspective in the leadership of the church. This immediately struck us as functionally egalitarianism, but we have since found that this line of thinking is pervasive in the modern church, even among supposedly conservative churches and institutions.

learn doctrine? This line of thinking neglects the fact that God has already appointed an office in the church to guard doctrine, instruct in theology and practice, and otherwise minister the Word: the male elders.

Male leadership, in the church and in marriages, is an enormous gift to the women in the flock and homes. Women are often much too empathetic toward one another, which is rarely a true help or solution to real problems. Husbands and elders are given true authority from the Lord to correct and lead through problems. If you believe this, you will find their teaching and correction to be valuable. You won't roll your eyes and automatically assume they are out of touch with your feminine needs and perspective. You won't dismiss their instruction as simply misunderstanding you or the problem. You will be quiet and listen. You will take care to weigh their words with respect and an eagerness to be instructed. This in turn tends to draw out the seriousness of their role in giving instruction; when a man's wife is eager to listen to and obey him, it puts a weight on him in a good way. He knows that his wife will do what he says—so he had better take his role seriously.

Refusing to be led spiritually by your husband in this way doesn't mean that the need to be led disappears. Be aware: You are being led by someone or something. If it's not your husband, then who or what is it? Are you letting your mother lead you? Some strange woman's social media account? Your emotions? Your friends? Sometimes it's important to cut off opinions and lines of communications from sources that aren't edifying you in the right way, especially if they're contradicting the wishes of your husband. I know I've chosen a trusted friend when I go to them for advice (with my husband's permission) and share the problem and they in turn ask, "What does your husband think?" Wise friends know they aren't the ultimate source of guidance in your walk and will respect your husband's leadership and authority.

This is why it's extremely important for women to guard their friendships. As a matter of fact, in his wonderful book *Face to Face*, Steve Wilkins says,

> God has so constituted us that we will become like our friends. "Do not enter the path of the wicked, and do not walk in the way of evil. Avoid it, do not travel on it; turn away from it and pass on" (Prov. 4:14–15). It is not merely advice; it is a command from God. You may not continually associate with evil men as friends, companions, or intimates; instead, you have an obligation to avoid them (26–27). If you notice a woman complaining about her husband or her friend's husbands, take note and avoid her. Proverbs 22:24–25 tells us we are not to make friends with angry women like this because they are a snare to our soul. If a snare to our soul, how much more to our marriages? Women are easily deceived (1 Tim. 2:14) and we will sometimes want to give them the benefit of the doubt, say they've had a hard life, and try to maintain intimate friendship anyways out of Christian charity, but Scripture tells us *not* to be deceived in such matters: "Bad company ruins good morals."[2]

In summary, remember that your husband is one of the tools God has ordained in the pursuit of your Christlikeness. He was given to you to make you more like Jesus. In fact,

---

2. *Face to Face: Meditations on Friendship and Hospitality* (Moscow, ID: Canon Press, 2010), 26–27.

the further along the road toward Christ you both travel together, the more like your true selves you will become—the true inner self whom Christ is bringing into being by His own sanctifying grace. There is almost no greater gift, short of watching your children grow in grace, than watching your spouse become more like Jesus and being one of the main recipients of such virtuous character.

CHAPTER 10

IN PRAISE OF
PRAISING YOUR
HUSBAND

I remember early on in our marriage expressing concern to my husband about yet another exposé of a prominent Christian leader in America who had fallen to disqualifying sin. We all know the story: A man thought he was above the rules, fell into sexual sin, and brought shame and ruin down on himself, his family, and his church. His public persona of holiness had proven a lie—a mask of piety hiding the real man beneath.

After agreeing with me about the shame of the news, my husband said something that has stuck with me. "Don't forget the hundreds of thousands of faithful men all over the world who actually are obeying the Lord and actually are being faithful to their wives and children. Those guys don't get congratulated. Their stories don't make the headlines. Nobody is writing news stories about their hard work and faithfulness."

It may sound strange, but this simple sentiment shook me. I hadn't actually considered these things from the perspective of a man. As I considered what my husband said, I realized that while it is universally normal to honor and praise women in our culture, it is rare to render honor to men in the same way. Women are often flattered; men rarely complimented at all. It's actually worse than this. Not only are men rarely praised, but when a man is doing his God-given duty of leading—of fighting for truth, the church, or his people—he's often called names for it, and even accused of being and doing horrible and untrue things. Bold leadership is slandered as domineering swagger. Strength is recast as sinful aggression. Single-minded focus on a task is seen as neglect or distraction. Emotional strength and resilience are made out to be a lack of care and proper concern. Men are urged, more or less, to try their best to become more like women, their unique glories scorned as evils. In short, our men are severely in need of a hearty word of encouragement, and we wives are in an excellent place to provide the help.

So, how does a lady learn to notice and praise those traits in her husband that are praiseworthy? It may feel awkward at first, especially if being bubbly isn't instinctual for you. Some women naturally think to give honor aloud; others find it embarrassing or challenging. If you find this to be hard, start by cultivating an awareness of that background cultural pressure *not* to praise your man that I just pointed out. Feministic folly is in the air we breathe. We are daily conditioned to think that the sharp and sarcastic woman wins in the head-to-head battle with her husband by her keen tongue. We think giving honor is weak. Recognize this cultural pressure, cast it off, and *do it anyway*. Learn to give him honor.

Beyond background cultural conditioning, it may also be simple, garden-variety sin that keeps you from opening your mouth to honor your husband. Maybe you are proud. Maybe your pride has concluded that your husband is your competition rather than your head. Maybe your pride has believed that life with your husband is a zero-sum game, that if he gets honor, you must get less—forgetting that you are his glory, the crown on his head, and that if he is elevated, so are you. Or maybe you are too shy. Did you know that there is such a thing as being *too* shy? Yes, some are naturally wired to be on the quieter end of the spectrum. But don't let shyness become sinful silence; shyness can sometimes be a cloak for simple unwillingness to humble yourself and honor another. There is such thing as inordinate shyness. It can be a genuine inhibitor to being a productive helper to your husband if you aren't willing to put yourself out there in any sort of way, be it for a hard conversation or a simple compliment.

Having said that, those who tend toward shyness may be happy to find that I am a hearty advocate of plain, ol' fashioned love letters and poems! Verbal praise isn't the only option for a wife to express honor. Why not share a journal of sweet encouragements that you pass back and forth between you and your husband? In such a format, you can take your time, not have to feel like you're on the spot, and say what you might feel awkward to say aloud. Sure, he may not be as expressive as you are, but why should that stop you from showering on the praise?

As wives, we have to take seriously our role as cheerleader in the home. Your husband likely spends all day at work being critiqued for his job. He likely has his own inner battle with thoughts of inadequacy, wondering if he is doing enough, working hard enough, providing enough. You don't want him to hesitate the moment he walks through the door out of fear of being served up an onslaught of complaints. There's no reason we can't learn from the housewives of yore who encouraged their tired husbands with a pretty face, a kind word, and maybe a hot drink or a snack when he got home. I don't think these are outdated whimsies to be scoffingly dismissed. These small acts add up to great big expressions of thankfulness and honor toward our husbands.

I'd like to add a warning here. It can be common in some circles for women, even Christian women, to get together and divulge unhelpful information or say rude things about their men behind their backs. It doesn't matter if what is said is true or untrue—this is simply sinful and unkind. It is also not the aid you may hope it to be in solving problems you may have with your husband. I believe that a woman should rarely be sharing marriage struggles with any other women unless she's been given permission by her husband, having spoken with him first. Though rare, there have been a few times where my husband and I are trying to work something out and I need to seek more counsel, but I always ask his permission first.

Obviously if you are being physically harmed by your husband (or you know someone in this situation), then you should seek help from the proper authorities, whether he wants you to or not. But let's be honest: That's different from thinking your husband is an idiot because he wants the kids in the private Christian school and you hate the idea, so you complain to all your friends about it at co-op. This is serious. Our husbands should be able to entrust themselves, their faults, and even their struggles with sin to us without being worried they will be blasted around the church all under the guise of prayer requests. Think about it; you would be so discouraged to find out your husband shared with his friends that he thinks you are too lazy to get dinner on the table on time. You wouldn't like it, so show him the same courtesy. Or how about a pastor airing all your private issues from a counseling meeting with dozens of others in the church? Such a thing would of course be wicked.

Don't get me wrong, I *have* counseled women who had genuine cause for concern in their marriages. But while it would be easy to simply say that women ought to always be ready to offer an empathetic hearing of each other's issues, such a practice would leave far too wide a doorway for sinful gossip and slander of our men in the guise of "sisterhood." Regular airing of grievances against our husbands to other ladies is simply not God's ordained means of help. As I've gotten older, I've realized that on my own I have very little authority to be of lasting help to women in hard marriages. I can offer a sympathetic ear and encourage them in their duties, but I firmly believe God has given *the elders* of the local church to be the primary counselors of the flock—and not just the men in the flock, but the women as well. Because of this, I don't spend a lot of time counseling women in these tricky situations, but rather point them to their pastors. These women need the wisdom and dedication of a trusted elder to help them walk through their marriage struggles. Godly elders are the ordained provision given to the local church to correct any regular patterns of sinful habits among the flock, and that includes between husbands and wives.

This protects the wife from sinning against her husband and running her mouth to any woman who will counsel her, and it protects the husband's honor so he isn't shamed before the church. If this paragraph offends you, I'd encourage you to consider more seriously the fact that it is a glory to cover over the offenses of others. It doesn't mean you don't work on getting the issue fixed; it just means you don't have to gratify the need to complain about it to people who really can't do anything to fix it. Are you "venting" simply to make yourself feel better for a few moments? Beware, sin crouches at your feet, ready to devour.

In our church and community, I am happy to say that this issue is very rare. I think this is at least in part due to the high and beautiful vision of biblical femininity that has been encouraged in the women in our local church. Against the backdrop of such a beautiful song, it feels immediately out of tune to hear a woman sing out her grievances with her husband to the wrong parties. Instead of needing to talk about the latest gossip, even the gossip of our own homes, we have found that cultivating a culture of readers has really helped mature and adorn the content of most conversations among our women. It's more normal to hear timeless ideas and connections being shared from the new books we are reading or funny stories that happened with our children than it is to hear grumbling and complaints. This isn't because our women haven't had their fair share of trials. In fact, some of the women in our midst who are the most hospitable and cheerful have been through some of the most heartbreak. They've taken the pain to the Healer and have allowed God to deal with them accordingly through the proper channels. The fruit is quite honestly astounding.

Instead of complaining to your friends about your man, I would encourage you to be diligent to find things to praise him for. Maybe he isn't the most articulate at family worship time, but did he come home to you last night? Did he pay the electricity bills? Were you able to buy groceries last week? Last month? Last year? Did he smile and kiss you in the morning even though you know you had coffee breath? Remember that you are an odd creature and hard to get along with sometimes too. Why is it that women only thank their husbands for the overtly romantic things: gifts, date nights, vacations? Maybe consider how romantic it is next time he hangs a picture for you and give him a hug and a smooch and rub his back for him that night. God often encourages men to grow into Christlike maturity by the women he has given them. If you actually *believe* and *say* he is an amazing, hardworking, faithful man, it will be hard for him to indulge in passivity at work because he won't want to let you down. You will often find that you tend to get more of what you honor, less of what you ignore or belittle.

"But you don't know how bad I have it."

It's true. I don't understand. I'm not writing this book from across your kitchen table. We've probably never met. I can speak to general principles, not your particulars. And so, in that spirit, here's the principle for hard times: Complaining to your husband, intentionally introducing distance between you and your husband, and withholding honor from your husband will almost never be a real solution to real problems. Why not try lavishing your man with heartfelt honor and praise and see what happens? Even if it doesn't make your husband change overnight, you know you are obeying the Lord in expressing a respectful attitude through your encouragement to your husband. A cheerful heart is good medicine, even for a difficult marriage, but a broken spirit dries up any life that was there. Pray that God would use your praise to encourage, equip, and embolden your husband to fight his sin and mature into Christlike masculinity.

CHAPTER 11

HIS GARDEN

"But *why*? How come *I* have to cook, *and* clean, *and* take care of the kids, *and* run the errands, *and* make sure everyone gets their violin homework done, *and* on top of all of it…do *that* on demand?" Is this how you feel about the marriage bed? Have you ever slipped into this kind of thinking or allowed yourself to feel this way? If so, this chapter is for you.

Being sexually hospitable to your husband is one of the good works the Lord has put in front of you to walk in. It's one of the things Paul is talking about in Ephesians 2:10 when he says that "We are his workmanship, created in Christ Jesus for good works, which God prepared beforehand, that we should walk in them." Maybe that sounds strange to you, but it's true! This becomes plain when we read something else Paul has to say, this time in 1 Corinthians 7:3–4: "The husband should give to his wife her conjugal rights, and likewise the wife to her husband. For the wife does not have authority over her own body, but the husband does. Do not deprive one another…"

When we consider these two passages together, we find

that good works are like footsteps. God doesn't call the Christian woman to a few acts of radical obedience at pivotal moments in her life, but to many acts of mundane and simple obedience every day and hour she has been given. Good works are footsteps, not events of historic magnitude—and as we see in 1 Corinthians 7, honoring the marriage bed with frequent sexual attention to your husband is one of those good works He has set before you.

So how can we grow in this good work? The first suggestion I have is to make time in your day to create little habits that you use to express your interest in and thankfulness for your husband. Some of you may need to literally write it down on your to-do list if it slips your mind regularly. But whatever your method, figure out how to reserve the time and energy in a regular way in your evening flow to go to your marriage bed with your husband with eagerness and warmth.

Second, consider your communication to your husband on this front as a whole, including your words, looks, texts, demeanor, and all the rest. We women are very good at communicating with our body language, sometimes communicating our truest feelings nonverbally even as we lie with our mouths: "I'm fine," you might say, even as your demeanor and body language say, "You can go fall in a ditch for all I care." That is obviously not the goal, right? So, it is important that we learn to express warmth, desire, and eagerness for our husband's affections with our words and demeanor. Ask yourself: Does the totality of my communication to my husband—verbal and nonverbal—express to him that I am his, that I desire him, and that I am eager to be his sole source of sexual satisfaction? Would he say that I communicate this spirit to him?

One issue that sometimes plagues women is the idea that they ought to be playing "hard to get" with their husbands. We seem skilled at this right out of the womb, but trust me, that's not what a faithful husband wants to come home to night after night. Women should be very, very hard to get, then very, very easy to get—hard to get in the sense of having high standards for a man to whom you will give yourself in marriage, but then easy to win by that worthy man who has won your heart and made his vows to you.

Once you're married, it shouldn't be an endless game of your husband having to "win your heart" again and again. Modern culture and media can present this view, as if the man should be constantly wining and dining his wife just to get a flicker of interest in return, but this is the height of folly. Remember the vows he took, the job he faithfully works, and count the other ways he cares for you and your family day in and day out as actual tokens of romance. Don't make your husband put extra-special romance coins in the slot to receive occasional affection in return. Instead, learn to see all his faithfulness and kindness to you as part of your romance: Your husband actually *is* expressing his love to you when he gets a paycheck every two weeks. He *is* being romantic when he gets new tires on the car before the snow hits. It *is* charming that he comes home to you—and you alone—night after night after night. Never take that for granted. Not all husbands come home to their wives every night. Obviously, we all like candlelight, massages, and small gifts from time to time, but you are being unrealistic if you are making your husband run through a hamster wheel of romantic exercises constantly to win you. You should be a faithful and steadfast wife yourself whose emotions are not ever-changing with the day of the month (yes, I do mean what you think I mean). Be steadfast, faithful to him, and unchanging in your affection for him, and see how firm his loyalty will prove to such a helper.

Part of your vocation as a wife is to be a source of marital joy, comfort, and protection to your husband. This isn't a task to be overlooked or considered only *after* you've gotten all the closets and cupboards in order. As a matter of fact, I promise your husband would rather the house be messier, more dishes left in the sink, or dinners be simpler if it makes you more sexually available to him. Don't be a martyr about this. Pray and ask the Lord to stir up genuine interest in your husband. Ask God for supernatural energy at the end of the day, if need be, or creativity to be sexually available at other times. Some seasons are harder than others. Whatever you do, do not make your husband feel like he's just another chore on your list to be crossed off so you can get on to more important things. That's not what I mean when I say that this is a part of your "vocation," as if it is to be turned into a task to be performed with the same spirit with which you vacuum the living room. If this genuinely is the mentality you are struggling with, you may need to open lines of communication with your husband, confess your distance, and maybe brainstorm together some ways you can free up your mental load to be more present. (In my experience, this usually requires the wife simply being disciplined enough in her thought life to let things go in order to be present with her husband.) Whatever you do, remember the goal is regular oneness in the marriage bed.

Again, be aware of your body language, because you are communicating to your husband how you really feel about him. When he tells you good morning at the kitchen sink, do you instinctively pull away? Or do you lean in and giggle a little? Are you cold? Do you make yourself scarce after dinnertime? Or do you go snuggle him on the couch? Do you let him show you physical affection, and give affection in return, in front of the kids? Do they know you have a crush on their daddy? Or do they just think you live with him so he has someone to iron his work shirts? Are you thinking regularly about how to show and tell him that you are his garden of delights? That you are his? That he has your heart and your affection?

It is also important to remember the golden rule of the Christian life, which is to do unto others what you would have them do unto you (Luke 6:31; Matt. 7:12). One paradox that women often miss when it comes to obeying these commands with respect to their marriage beds becomes clear when we pause and ask the question: What does my husband want from me on this front? Men and women are not identical. He has to know what you desire in order to properly love you, and you need to know what he desires to properly love him. He needs to know that as a woman, you need safety, care, attention, gentleness, and affection. You need to know that he seeks respect, honor, and interest from you. When it comes to the marriage bed, one thing this means is that you need to understand that your husband wants to win you, to impress you, to woo you. He doesn't just want you to be a passive and uninterested recipient of his sexual affection, but an active and interested party. He wants to please *you*, not just himself. What does this mean for you? One thing it means is that you ought to cultivate an eagerness to *be* pleased by your husband just as much as to please him. Be easy to win. Be easy to woo. Be easy to delight.

Finally, my husband often says that the spouse with the higher sex drive should set the pace of the marriage—and I agree. This makes sense if we remember that part of the purpose of marriage is to sanctify each spouse on their journey toward heaven. Stewarding the good gift that is your marriage bed is extremely sanctifying to many women, especially in a feminist world awash with the lie that women don't owe their men a single thing. Shut your ear to that garbage; it is toxic wickedness. If your sex life was only about you and what *you* wanted (or didn't want) all the time, that wouldn't require much Christlikeness of you, would it? Maybe it seems embarrassing to you, too earthy to you, but God really did design sex and all its goodness as a means of making you more like His Son. How cool is that? God delights in our delight in one another, for it was His creation from the beginning—so be sure to delight in your husband to the glory of your Maker.

CHAPTER 12

BITTER WATERS

Both husbands and wives need to be aware that it is possible to stumble your spouse by wanting to talk an issue over to unnecessary lengths. It is possible to overthink a problem, to let it consume your thoughts and words and heart until it is all-consuming. There may be discord and sin between your family and a family that sits beside you in the pews every week. Your husband may have taken some concerns he's seeing in the flock to the elders, and it didn't go well. You may have relational conflict with a friend that is eating you up and doesn't seem close to resolution. Wives, please know that one of the worst things you can do in situations like this is talk the details to death with your husband, to let it dominate your thoughts and words unnecessarily.

Why? Isn't he supposed to be your head? Your leader and confidante? Yes, those things are true. But to put it simply, harboring the expectation of repeatedly replaying every detail of a problem may be laying a giant trap before your husband. It is not wise for *anyone* to turn over and revisit every detail of a hard circumstance time and time again. You may be watering roots of bitterness in your husband that he now has to dig out of his heart, in addition to trying to navigate an already hard circumstance with wisdom. As a rule, women are often tempted to over-talk issues, neglecting to cultivate the ability to soberly assess a problem, determine what the Lord would have them do about it, and then entrust it to him without anxiety or a constant need to turn it over in their minds and in conversation.

For some marriages, this may mean a wife has to regularly be okay with being in the dark about certain details of problems her husband is working through. Sure, the husband should fill her in as necessary, but if he returns from each meeting needing to have his five-page report in hand, wisdom and self-control are probably lacking somewhere. Something I've had to learn over the years as a pastor's wife is that my primary goal when my husband gets home— especially from very spiritually or relationally difficult meetings—is to simply be a source of refreshment to him. Is it late? Does he need some back scratches to relax? Did the meeting go an hour and a half past dinner and he really just needs a plate of pasta and a cookie and not a list of questions from me? Great! I am happy to be his helper and not his interrogator.

In my experience, meeting your husband's needs as a helper and *then* asking questions later is the best way to go about gaining the most needful information in a way that helps everyone involved. This takes some spiritual maturity on a wife's part, but it is good that she learn to defer her questions, fears, and anxieties.

Let's consider a circumstance unrelated to church life: A husband and wife may have discussed a husband taking a bold chance and talking to his boss about switching to a higher-paying position at a different branch of his company. The husband knows that truthfully, he isn't entirely qualified on paper, but he's hoping that his years of faithful and hard work as unto the Lord will give him favor in the boss's eyes. The wife may be very excited about the prospect for many reasons. She knows how hard he works and believes he can handle more responsibility, some extra cash would make it easier to get the kids new instruments in the fall, and having another baby wouldn't look so daunting to the bank account if he got a raise.

A wife can be excited and pray that the Lord would prosper her husband's boldness, but after her husband proposes this idea to her, I'd encourage her to be careful to not bring up the idea every chance she has. In short, she shouldn't get her hopes up. She needs to be able to be a source of encouragement to her husband. If she's so worked into a flurry of anxiety and fear about maybe not getting what she wants out of the deal, her husband will not only have to deal with the challenging situation and his own potential disappointments, but also figure out how to deal with hers as well.

I came across an interesting section in Zechariah 12:12 where God tells the husband and wives to mourn separately. This is an example of this same principle in Scripture. Husbands and wives are responsible as individuals before the Lord for their reactions. Yes, the wife is also in the husband's realm of responsibility, but she is genuinely an individual before the Lord who will give an account for her own sin.

Maybe husbands need to coach their wives in this way. Don't be offended if your husband tells you before leaving for a big meeting, "Let's not talk about this tonight. We can talk about it tomorrow while we go for a walk with the kids." Or he may start a conversation with, "I'm going to share these details with you, but after we talk about it, I don't want to talk about it over and over again." This is not him trying to smother your feelings, but trying to protect and help you and probably himself as well. Remember, you want a man of integrity, and sometimes that means having a man who will tell you, "We don't need to discuss this anymore. Let's entrust it to God and do what we know He has called us to do."

A good friend of mine was recently sharing what a strong leadership position her husband took in their church and family when some fallout started between the elders and members in the congregation. "My husband told me we are not partaking in any gossip." It was obvious from the entire conversation that the husband had protected her from falling into sin with foolish women. I could see that it allowed them to listen to both sides of the story and more accurately assess and help those involved. Fretful gossip isn't just something that happens outside the walls of your home. It is a very real sin to fall into at your own dinner table with your own family members.

"But Lexy, you've admitted women are designed to be communicators. What am I supposed to do then?"

First, trust that your husband will share pertinent details, understanding that often we need to know much less than we think we do. Sure, it's not a gratifying delicious morsel (Prov. 18:8), but it's really the Lord's perspective that we need to get on the situation, not all the juiciest details. And let's be honest, knowing every single word and exchange that happened between your husband and his boss doesn't change your day-to-day duties. The information is not as necessary as you think it is.

Next, have you gotten in your prayer closet and poured out your concerns to the Lord? I often find that when I do that first, I am much less fretful when it comes to discussing details of a conflict or stressful situation with my husband. I can handle hard circumstances and unexpected trials without crying because I've already mourned before the Lord. I don't take offense when I hear a lie someone has spread about me because I have the Lord's protection. Prayer equips me to turn a profit on hard circumstances by allowing me to process the trial with the Lord and learn to rejoice in Him even amid the hardship.

When this goes wrong in a marriage, I have seen men who are more worried about offending their wives than they are about leading well and guarding their homes from gossip. The wives too often fill that leadership void, manipulating their husbands with bitterness and complaining. Their husbands, wearied of their fussing, can fall into a sinful failure to lead and allow the fussing to continue instead. This weakens everyone in the family and often drives every member of it, including the children, into isolation. The gossiping, complaining, drama-obsessed, and drama-creating wife—combined with a weak husband who won't rein her in—leads the family to constant friction with every church and community they join. They end up isolated and wandering. Children growing up in homes like this, isolated from robust Christian community, are then lacking in examples of helpful and respectful Christian communication in marriage, perpetuating the problem down through the generations. Maybe your job is to break this cycle in your family. Maybe your mother and father were like this. Understand this: It really can stop with you. The Lord is on your side.

Instead of offering our husbands bitter waters on the home front, let's make it our goal that our tables and living rooms and bedrooms would be places of sweet refreshment and self-control. Practically speaking, this might look like cooking an extra-festive meal on the weeks when your husband or family receives bad news. It might mean getting out the candles and planning a romantic night in for just the two of you when the gossip train seems extra loud and cacophonous. Even in trials and conflict, you have extraordinary power as your husband's helper to make his home a place of warmth and cheer. May you become the type of woman whose husband can always trust you to do him good and not harm all the days of his life.

CHAPTER 13

ON WAITING IT OUT

Let's talk about everyone's favorite subject: patience. Particularly, patience in the face of angst. Here's what I mean, the thesis of this chapter: Rarely is it a good idea to immediately bring up a conversation topic that has you feeling angsty. Instead, take the time to carefully consider the situation objectively, organize your thoughts, and then act with the wisdom of forethought. Every bit of your reasoning may be trying to convince you otherwise: "He *needs* to know right now! Today! This evening! This really *can't* wait. It's up to *you* to inform him! You are his helper, after all!"

These all can be very real motivators in talking to your husband about a variety of issues in a timely manner. Some things really are pressing. But it's also true that sometimes you need to sit on things for a bit. Sometimes you need to wait it out, take time to pray, and not vent your feelings or anxieties as quickly as possible. Now, when I say "sit on things," I don't mean shoving them down until you burst out in anger, frustration, feelings of neglect, or any other yucky feelings. When I am internally sitting on a topic, I'm taking my pleas to God for help in my time of need. Here are a few things I've gleaned by not oversharing my emotions, thoughts, or concerns with my husband too quickly and instead praying about them.

New information often shows up. Sometimes I am simply annoyed by something and maybe I want to feel validated by sharing with my husband. I want him to understand and maybe justify my thoughts a bit more. The problem is that I've learned many times I've simply reacted to misinformation. Or entirely new information may show up, totally resolving my complaint or worry all on its own. I am often grateful that the Lord has helped me keep my mouth shut in such circumstances, because I know I would have wasted energy and time, precious resources, and caused a bother over something that was likely outside of both my and my husband's hands.

How I was feeling was wrong. As a general rule, if something in your spirit is pressing you to burst out in haste, be suspicious. Our feelings often overrun wisdom and must be ruled over by the will. Allowing your emotions to spur you on to hasty outburst with regularity is not a virtue, but a vice. Rather than being *reactive*, the mature Christian woman should strive to be *proactive*—setting the thermostat of her own emotions. "I know this unexpected issue that just popped up is a big inconvenience, but I'm simply not allowed to lash out at the kids all afternoon because of this. God has given me authority over my own emotions in the home. They are not in charge. I can be a kind mother in the face of inconvenience and overlook this." Your internal temperature can be set to godly behavior, so that even when the weather outside is howling and storming, there is peace and calm inside the home.

The older I get, the more I realize the virtue of mentally pausing to think through difficult or emotionally laden information and then consider the presentation of what I'd like to say and what details to leave out or include, and only then to speak. I've found it helpful to use a mental checklist like this to make sure my words are truly going to edify my listener. When I do this with something I want to discuss with my husband, I often realize I am overreacting and being too emotional. If there is truthfully something that still needs to be shared, but I sit on the information and pray through it first, I am almost always able to communicate effectively and come to an agreement with my husband. But giving myself the time to mull things over has protected me on many occasions from sinning in my reactions. Taking that time allows you to pray and get right with the Lord so you can stay in fellowship with your spouse. This is not always easy, but it is something you will learn with diligent practice as you grow in maturity. Children give full vent to their spirit without restraint. Mature and godly women do not.

When I find out new information about the situation and I'm able to maturely assess how I should be feeling, I have regularly come to realize that my original solution wasn't right after all. An example may be that you realize next weekend is your anniversary. Due to your own forgetfulness, you may have projected onto your husband that he likely forgot as well. You have a low-grade feverish feeling of annoyance all afternoon as you chop vegetables and knead the dough. "He probably isn't even planning anything at all," you tell yourself through gritted teeth. You set your face to flat mode when he walks in the door. You stiffen a bit when he leans in to kiss you. When he pulls out your chair for dinner, he says, "Oh, honey! Our anniversary is next Saturday night! My mom is going to watch the kids so we can go out. Be thinking about where you'd like to go."

If you're like me in a similar circumstance, you immediately feel regret that you've been so selfish and rude—even if only in your thoughts—toward your husband. Experiences like this in marriage are very humbling to me. They often cause me to be extremely grateful for my husband. God has used this embarrassment to warn me against falling into that same sin again when faced with similar circumstances in the future. "Don't forget how silly you acted last time!"

Other times, as I quietly pray over a situation, God divinely intervenes, demonstrating that He is the Great Problem Solver. I've seen it happen through many means—softening and changing of people's hearts, miraculous provision, or working out circumstances that were outside of my control. He often acts in ways I neither foresaw nor controlled in any way. I think God delights to do this for us to teach us to trust in His strength rather than our own hands.

When God is the One to show up and move like this, I am also reminded that prayer is a powerful tool in the Christian wife's tool belt. I have often been concerned about something in my marriage or our family life and I will take my concerns and worries to the Lord. I may be saying something like, "I don't like what I'm seeing here. I don't want to be a nag. Please change his heart. Show him this is wrong." Often God will move in my husband's heart and he will come to me in agreement with the concerns I've had, as well as already having worked out a solution. After seeing this again and again, I have learned to remind myself that when I want to start to nag my husband about something,

I had better start praying and let the Holy Spirit be the one doing the correcting. It's a much more effective and lasting approach.

Proverbs 18:17 demonstrates the principle that there is wisdom in hearing out both sides of a story. It is to our shame when we are unwilling to do the investigatory work owed to our loved ones. While you wait it out, you should actively figure out the truth of the circumstantial information you happened upon. You may be prone to making judgment calls and jumping to conclusions about your husband's behavior. If you respond too quickly, you are likely to react in anger and do harm that you'll need to repent of down the road. I do believe it's okay to wait and ask questions of your spouse to gather more information, as long as you can do it in a non-accusatory way.

For example, let's say that your husband had a meeting cancel at work and decided to come home early and surprise you with an offer to go take the family out for dinner and ice cream, but you already had dinner cooked and a lot of work to get done at home. You *shouldn't* say something like, "So you think all I have to do is sit and wait around for you all day? Because if so, you're wrong, *Buck-o!* I already made dinner, and I have three loads of laundry to do. You never plan ahead." You could respond in a much more polite way, maybe more like this: "I'm glad you were able to change your schedule around! What happened to your meeting? I had a lot of chores planned for today, but I'm thankful you thought of us and made time to hang out. I'll put the dinner I made in the fridge for tomorrow instead and we can all have a fun evening together."

Part of a willingness to hear your husband's side of the

story comes from being charitable toward him. I am always so astonished at how charitable my husband is toward people who have purposefully misrepresented him, attacked him, or otherwise sought his harm. It used to bother me, but I've learned to really value it as a godly character trait. A charitable wife assumes the *best* about her husband, not the worst. You can see how this changes your entire approach to a problem. "He is so sweet and thoughtful! He probably didn't realize this would be a slight inconvenience to my work this week. I'm thankful he likes to spend time with me and the kids." This is much more charitable than complaining and being annoyed about your ever-growing errand list while you sit beside your husband at dinner. "*Ugh.* It's just because he feels bad he's going out of town next week. He didn't *really* take me here because he just wanted to be with me. Now I have even *more* work to figure out how to tackle while he's gone."

Do yourself a favor and don't allow yourself to speak slanderously about your husband, even if it's just in your thought life. Proverbs 19:11 says that good sense makes one slow to anger, that it is a glory to overlook an offense. Doesn't this show us how idiotic it is to become easily ruffled? It is a woman's glory to look over an offense, especially such small (or entirely made up) offenses. I've found that the people with the biggest marriage problems are often the ones who refuse to overlook the most minuscule of offenses in the other person. They are easily ruffled. And since they never cultivated a meek spirit in little ways, when it came to the big problems, their muscles weren't there to help them carry the glorious weight of being a woman with a gracious, forgiving disposition. Some of the biggest fights were fought over the silliest things, like someone forgetting to take out the trash. With Christ's help, we really can resolve to be understanding and gracious communicators.

CHAPTER 14

A HUSBAND FORGETS TO FOLLOW UP

I've had many conversations in which a wife asks me what she should do when her husband has forgotten to follow up on something he promised to do. Often these women genuinely don't want to be a nag. They feel like reminding him too many times may be entering the realm of leaky roof territory (Prov. 27:15), and they rightly want to avoid that. These women don't want to drive their husbands to take up residence on the corner of their own roofs (Prov. 21:9), but they also really do need some things taken care of that only he can do. What to do?

Let's start with some baseline principles: A good husband will generally not micromanage his wife. His heart will trust her with the details of their life, family, marriage, and household—and because of this, some husbands may not dip their hands into the detail pot of the ins and outs of domestic life at home. My husband schedules his own reminders on his calendar, but he also regularly asks me to remind him of a variety of things. I will ask wives who come to me with this question if they have already expressed to their husband their need for help with the forgotten task. If they haven't, then I tell them to cheerfully and encouragingly initiate that conversation. Often, when a husband hears that his respectful and pleasant wife really needs his help to get something done, it's as good as done in his book. What man is not drawn to want to help his pleasant, respectful wife, after all? In many cases, such a wife will find that her husband has simply forgotten, that he is just as prone to normal human foibles as she is.

If a wife finds herself in the second boat, the forgetful-husband boat, my advice at this point is to remind her of her role as helper. I have learned in my own marriage that because my husband has an entire list of duties, job descriptions, tasks to remember, and many other things to accomplish at his places of work, he simply has a harder time remembering things that we've talked about him doing for the family and home. He isn't mentally pitting the importance of home life or marriage against the importance of his work. In fact, I have to remember that my husband excelling in his job actually *is* part of the goal of our household and marriage; he's not neglecting the home in working hard outside of it. That is one of the chief ways he *does* build up our home.

So even though it's an easy temptation, when my husband lets something fall through the cracks at home, I've had to coach myself to remember that it doesn't mean he doesn't love me. Further, I remind myself that this is part of why God has called me to *help* him. My husband regularly invites me to *help* him remember to do family worship after dinner, *help* him remember to get our vacation on the calendar, *help* him remember that he was going to get the kids signed up for next season's sport. In some ways I wonder if a husband's forgetfulness is simply God's way of creating dependence on one another in the marriage. It's plain fact that there are many tasks I need my husband's help with. In our home, this would be things like car issues and financial organization. But he also needs me to come alongside him and give him encouraging reminders, and I often help him wrap up loose ends on many projects. I am happy to be the footman when he is already carrying such a heavy load providing for our household.

"But I shouldn't have to remind him I need help with the dinner dishes! Isn't it obvious from the putrid smell coming from the sink!?"

What is obvious to women just isn't obvious to men. And it's very unkind to assume they've grown telepathy muscles overnight. Put yourself in his shoes. He's been working hard all day and is so grateful to be home, fed delicious food, and just can't wait for the change of pace that wrestling toddlers brings after a day at the office. Most likely he isn't trying to defraud you of help. He's just thoroughly enjoying his kids and his home.

So, what would I do about the dishes? Well, if it were me, I'd probably cheerfully do them myself. Then after the kids were tucked in and I was able to catch up with my husband one on one—as long as I wasn't angry about who got to sit on the couch after dinner or otherwise grumping about the issue—I'd simply say, "You've told me before to just ask for help when I need it, so here I am taking your advice. You mentioned you'd help pitch in to get the table cleared and get dishes in the dishwasher after dinner. Can you help with that after dinners? Would it be helpful if all the kids stayed behind and everyone pitched in? That way we could all go sit on the couch together and read stories." I always like to try to get ahead of the problem by providing at least one viable solution, showing that I, too, am willing to serve. If you're always looking for ways to take, that's usually a sign that you're being demanding or unreasonable in your request.

"But if I constantly have to remind him of things, isn't that a bit childish of him?"

Stop painting things in the worst possible light or wording things in the worst possible way. Women are prone to do this. *A lot*. Be aware and stop this toxic habit. Again, rejoice in the fact that God made you and your husband different ... and that this is a *good* thing. God knew what he was doing when He did it this way. Men and women are indispensable to each other, and women are not the superior sex. Men are not defective women, waiting for you to fix them by making them more naturally attentive to domestic maintenance like you are. Even if you *do* have to go the rest of your marriage reminding your husband of things he's requested your help in remembering, you will be a much happier woman having done so with a cheerful, gracious attitude than constantly acting like a soggy mop, sloshing bitterness and annoyance everywhere. My husband tells spouses who are at odds that even if the other person never changes or never remembers to do the thing they said they would do without a reminder, they can still get along if they will each do the hard work of patiently loving one another across small frustrations. In fact, God will often use the patience of the offended spouse as the very means by which the desired change ultimately occurs—not nagging, rudeness, or bitterness, but patience.

Chapter 15

The Mechanics of Staying in Fellowship

I think most of us have wished from time to time that we could be a fly on the wall in the homes of those with godly and mature families and marriages. We want to see what it looks like to overcome sin in real time, to work through issues in real time, to get back in fellowship after some minor annoyance or even a major issue in real time. This is really at the heart of most marriage issues—not knowing how to get into and remain *in* fellowship. Not knowing how to make it hard to get *out* of fellowship. These topics constitute some of the most regular conversations my husband and I have had when counseling young married couples and parents: how to maintain fellowship with one another and how to get *back* in fellowship with each other once it has been broken through sin.

For some people, it genuinely is the hardest thing in the

world to admit wrong, confess sin, and ask to be forgiven without having a ten-point argument as to why what they did really was necessary, or not their fault, or all just a big misunderstanding. I think there are a few reasons for this: The first and most obvious is simply that some people are proud and don't know how to take full responsibility for themselves. They constantly want to shift blame in order to make themselves feel better.

Another reason has to do with a lack of overt teaching on the topic. If you are a first-generation Christian and grew up in a dysfunctional environment, your heart may genuinely long for godly fellowship in the home, but you just don't have the handholds to get there. When I talk to people like this, they are often extremely humble and willing to take responsibility for themselves. They usually just need a bit of coaching as to how to confess their sin and seek restoration with those living under their roofs. They simply haven't seen it done. Nobody has ever taught them these basic things. Let's talk about some of the basics.

Though we are always growing in this skill ourselves in our family, there are a few things we regularly do that help tidy up the sin messes and deal with them fully. First off, as you have probably gathered from other chapters, know that it is never going to be easy or comfortable when you know you need to confess your sin. Don't wait for some emotional high to happen. Don't wait until you feel like it. Confess quickly and as publicly as you committed the sin. Did you mouth off at your husband in front of the kids while getting the hot dishes on the table for dinner? Once you've sat down, open your mouth and say in front of everyone, "Honey, that was an unnecessary comment that I made. I

shouldn't have said it that way. I am sorry for being disrespectful. Do you forgive me?"

I think a huge reason people often fail in this very first
step is because they think it's unnecessary. "What's the big
deal? Nobody's perfect. And I think they forgive me. They
got over it last time." But Proverbs 28:13 tells us that "whoever conceals his transgressions will not prosper, but he who
confesses and forsakes them will obtain mercy." Confessing
our sin isn't just about what the other person thinks. It's also
about our own standing before the Lord. Do you want to be
shown mercy? Then confess your sins and admit you *need*
mercy!

If you sinned against your spouse in private, perhaps
showing them the cold shoulder while you were out on a
date together, then go to them in private and confess. "I am
sorry I was rude all night. Do you forgive me?"

It may be okay from time to time to say something addi-
tional like, "It was a long week with all the doctor's appoint-
ments we had to get to, and I feel extra tired." However,
be sure to communicate something like, "But that really
doesn't matter. It wasn't right for me to be rude to you just
because I need a nap. It's still sin. Do you forgive me?"

Something to be avoided at all costs is saying something
like this: "I am sorry I was rude tonight, but I really don't
think you understand how hurt I am by what you did last
week. I'm trying to get over it, but you really don't seem to
understand."

Why should this be avoided? Because you are keeping a
record of wrongs. You are making it seem like we are allowed
to sin so long as someone else sinned, too—or even if someone just hurt your feelings. Instead, love would choose to

believe and hope all things, including telling yourself something like, "My husband is a godly man. He probably didn't realize how hurtful his behaviors were. I talked to him about it, and he apologized and said he will strive to not do that again and I am going to choose to believe him and not treat him as if he's guilty. I'm also going to love him by squashing these temptations I keep having to think ill of him." Loving someone should really change the way we think and act toward them, especially when it's your spouse. It is so common for women to have to fight the temptation to think slanderously about their husbands.

You should also avoid confessing things that aren't sin. For example, don't say, "I am sorry I am distracted tonight," or, "I am sorry I've been so tired this week." Think biblically about your sin so you can have effective biblical solutions. Being tired and distracted isn't a sin, but allowing tiredness and distraction to cause you to ignore your husband entirely or treat him with coldness *is* a sin, and it's called being rude. Love is not rude. If you were rude—regardless of *why*—that was the sin. You really do need to get good at analyzing the way you are thinking about things in this kind of reasoned, objective, and clear way if you want to be a Christian woman who can take responsibility for herself and maintain fellowship in the home. If you can't or won't do this, it will be hard for your loved ones to be around you the longer you go on in this stubborn way.

A lot of people are willing to admit wrong, but they don't want to be the first to do it. When I am tempted to do this, I know I need to remedy the situation as soon as possible. I don't wait until my husband gets home tonight to do this, giving me an entire day to ruminate and double down on my emotions. Instead, I pick up the phone, give him a call, and confess quickly. Trust me, I have had to do exactly this before! Ladies, to do this, you really do need to grow and exercise muscles that allow you to act contrary to your emotions. Be the first to roll over in bed and confess, the first to wander back to the other in the store and ask for forgiveness. Don't be stubborn. Don't be proud. Don't keep a detailed list of who repented first in your last 50 fights to make sure you never end up going first too often.

Practice makes perfect. I don't know if confessing our sins to each other will ever feel natural. But I do know that the more you grow the muscle and experience the joy of walking in the light together in your marriage, the faster you will want to restore fellowship, because God won't let you be content in your sin. Would you rather admit you were wrong and enjoy snuggling your husband on the couch tonight, or spend the evening alone in your room pouting? If you gave your husband the cold shoulder all morning, would you rather pick up the phone and ask for forgiveness the moment you realize you sinned, or huff about the house, vacuuming in a flurry of frustration and grumbling all day until he gets home from work?

It's not easy. We're talking about crucifying the flesh along with its passions and desires. The flesh *wants* to be out of fellowship. It *wants* to be proudly vindicated, to justify itself, and to win. But the Lord wants you to be humbled, to be righteous and eager to be at peace insofar as it's up to you. Don't shirk the development of this hard, good work. God can and will help you grow in these godly affections.

CHAPTER 16

MEEKNESS

If you don't regularly read the Puritans, you should consider adding them to the list. Set apart from much of modernity and post-Christian thought, and deeply steeped in the Scriptures, the Puritan body of literature is among the most practical and convicting works you could take up and read. I have several favorite titles that I revisit often, but *The Quest for Meekness and Quietness of Spirit* by Matthew Henry is one of the most helpful I've ever read. It's probably informed more of my views of communication in marriage than I'm even aware of. I come across convicting passages and remember, "Ohhhh, that's where I got that principle from!" I've read it many times at this point and in a variety of seasons, and every time I read it, I find fresh insight.

I find it so helpful that I wanted to conclude this short book by providing a few formative quotes just to give you a little taste of Henry's relevancy to the topic of marriage and communication. Meekness can be applied to pretty much any circumstance a Christian woman can find herself in, but it is particularly relevant to the Christian wife in pursuing godliness in her role.

I'll include my own comments on the passage so you can see how I practically turn quotes like these into cheat codes in the midst of highly volatile conversations, or when I feel tempted to sin with my attitude toward my husband.

Meekness is easiness for it accommodates the soul to every occurrence, and so makes a man easy to himself and to all about him.

In reference to our own anger, when at any time we meet with the excitement of it, the work of meekness is to do four things:

To consider the circumstances of that which we apprehend to be a provocation, so as at no time to express our displeasure, but upon due and mature deliberation. This office of meekness is to keep reason upon the throne in the souls as it ought to be, to preserve the understanding clear and unclouded, the judgment untainted and unbiased in the midst of the greatest provocations, so as to be able to set everything in its true light and to see it in its own color, and to determine accordingly, as also to keep silence in the court that the still small voice in which the Lord is (as he was with Elijah at Mount Horeb, 1 Kings 19:12, 13) may not be drowned by the noise of the tumult of the passions. A meek man will never be angry at a child, at a servant, at a friend till he has first seriously weighed the cause in just and even balance, while a steady and impartial hand holds the scales, and a free and unprejudiced thought judges it necessary.

This passage cuts straight to the heart in the middle of the heat. I think many people misunderstand a meek person as one who may be silly, uneducated, and easy to manipulate or walk all over, but this passage shows the strength and intellect of meekness. Being a godly, meek character requires you to be willing to grow in logic and justice, because you aren't easily pushed around by your emotions or the emotions of others, but instead know what it means to be reasonable and truthful about the circumstances.

Hear reason, keep passion silent, and then you will not find it difficult to bear the provocation.

This may be the easiest to remember and most helpful practical tip from the entire book. Ladies, when you begin to feel tempted to throw a barb with your words, "keep passion silent." Literally, cover your mouth if you have to. Bite your tongue.

In every cause, when passion demands immediate judgment, meekness moves for further time and will have the matter fairly argued, and counsel heard on both sides.

I think it's important to admit we often want immediate solutions. We want our side heard *now*. We want details corrected *now*. We want justice done on our behalf *now*. The fact is that God knows the truth, and because of that we should not always *have* to finish the argument before bed, or in front of the guests, or at all. It is a mark of maturity to be able to keep your mouth shut, pray on the topic, and bring it up at a more constructive time, or not at all if it is something you need to overlook.

＊

Meekness teaches and enables us patiently to bear the anger of others...Commonly, that which provokes anger is anger, as fire kindles fire; now meekness prevents that violent collision which forces out these sparks, and softens at least one side, and so puts a stop to a great deal of mischief; for it is the second blow that makes the quarrel.

Learn to overlook the offense and not make the second blow. Many, many quarrels could be avoided if this advice were heeded. But why not defend yourself? Our silence shouldn't be viewed as a sign of giving up, but rather as a means of making room for the justice and wrath of God in the circumstances.

＊

If the heart be angry, angry words will but inflame it the more, as wheels are heated by a rapid motion. One reflection and repartee begets another, and the beginning of the debate is like the letting forth of water which is with difficulty stopped when the least breach is made in the dam; therefore meekness says, "By all means keep silence, and leave it off before it be meddled with."....

Those who find themselves wronged and aggrieved think they may have permission to speak, but it is better to be silent than to speak amiss and make work for repentance. At such a time, he that holds his tongue holds his peace; and if we soberly reflect we shall find we have been often the worst for our speaking, but seldom the worse for our silence.

She who holds her tongue holds her peace. Remember this.

A soft answer is the dictate and dialect of that wisdom which is from above, which is "peaceable, gentle, and easy to be entreated."

Do you consider it *wise* to be peaceable? Do you make it easy for others to be at peace with you? Or do you create mental and physical obstacle courses for your husband to run through to prove his love to you? Women manipulate in lots of ways: with their bodies, bank accounts, and the atmosphere in the homes. We should strive to be women whose feet run to make peace with others, not women whose feet run to mischief and manipulation.

CLOSING ENCOURAGEMENT FROM THE AUTHOR'S HUSBAND

by Brian Sauvé

The wounds of a friend are faithful, indeed—though that doesn't mean they aren't wounds. Wounds hurt. Sometimes just a brief sting, but sometimes they hurt with a deep and lasting pain. As a pastor, I have been the deliverer of many friendly wounds; this is often what it means, after all, to minister the Word of God to people. The Word of God is a mirror, relentlessly calling us to look into its reflection and see there two things: the image of the perfect man, Jesus Christ, and the image of our own imperfect selves. This is, of course, a part of God's love for us—to drive us to his throne of grace for mercy and help, that we might be both saved from our sin and transformed from one degree of glory to another into the image of Christ.

One thing the Scriptures demand is that older women in the faith teach the younger women to love their husbands and children, to bring their homes to the flourishing and warmth of a man and a woman living out the gospel parable with joy and with zeal. This book has been full of just that—wisdom for those with ears to hear on the journey toward households like that. But that said, some of it may have hurt your feelings. Maybe at various points you found yourself arguing with Lexy in your head. Maybe you felt the sting of correction here, the jolt of shame there, or even the deep cut of rebuke. Let me conclude this book with three exhortations to you, sisters, from the husband of the author:

First, remember the gospel of Jesus Christ. What do we do when correction cuts? When it wounds? We run to the cross. We shelter there. We confess our sins and cast ourselves on the mercy of God. We remember that the solution to our sins does not lie in our ability to merely clean ourselves up, adopt a few new habits of moral reform, and then call it good. No, we need *forgiveness.* And so, the very first thing I would urge you to do with any conviction these pages may have brought to you is to *be clean.* Look to Christ with thanksgiving, for He has washed our scarlet sins as white as snow.

Second, don't wait. Remember, the conviction of the Spirit is a part of God's love for us. It is meant to lead us to repentance, life, joy, and restoration. So don't wait. Don't wait to turn from that sin; create and walk in new habits of grace and holiness, and apply what you've learned. Knowledge is a dangerous thing, isn't it? It can give us the illusion of maturity. You might believe that simply *knowing* you must respect your husband means you *are* respecting your husband. You might begin to believe that being able to give a lengthy discourse on the cultural damage done by all the various waves of feminism means you are a virtuous and godly woman. You may be deceived, thinking that all the books you've read on having a gentle and quiet spirit means that you automatically have one.

But we know this isn't how maturity works. Maturity is found in the living, not the knowing. It certainly *requires* knowing, but knowing alone won't do it. In fact, knowing may serve only to heap the sin of hypocrisy atop the sins of the nagging and reviling wife. So don't wait. Where the Spirit corrected you in the pages of this book, get concrete, make a plan, and start putting one foot in front of the other to walk in those good works God has laid before your feet.

Third and finally, beware the everything-perfect-right-now-or-I-give-up fallacy. Did I just make this fallacy up? Yes. Yes, I did. But I think it's a good one. The everything-perfect-right-now-or-I-give-up fallacy is exactly what it sounds like: thinking that unless you can do every single thing right now, that unless you can repent of all the sins all the way right this second, that you may as well give up. Yes, you may have a mountain of repentance to do. Maybe you have been a nagging, disrespectful, rude wife, totally lacking in self-control. Maybe you have let your emotions drag you around the mud like a tin can tied behind a 600-lb pig with a particularly vigorous exercise routine.

That may be true. And you may feel overwhelmed. Maybe you have a to-do list that is dozens of points long from reading this book. Here's my counsel to you: Don't give up. Don't be overwhelmed. Pick the biggest, nastiest, smelliest, rottenest sin on the list, and get to work killing that one first. Then the next one. And the next after that. Is the Lord God not on your side? Did Christ not die for those exact sins and rise for your life? Did He not put His Spirit in you? Do you not have a new heart in your chest? Is God not taking you to glory?

Go and live like He is...because He is. Close this book with this blessing from the Lord:

> The LORD bless you and keep you;
> the LORD make his face to shine upon you and be
> gracious to you;
> the LORD lift up his countenance upon you and give
> you peace.
> (Num. 6:24–26)

And amen.

SCRIPTURE INDEX

OLD TESTAMENT

New Testament

About the Author

LEXY SAUVÉ is married to her high school sweetheart, Brian, and together they have seven kids. She co-hosts Bright Hearth, a podcast devoted to the productive Christian household.